Soccer
Skills & Drills

National Soccer Coaches Association of America

Jim Lennox
Director of Coaching Emeritus, NSCAA

Janet Rayfield
University of Illinois

Bill Steffen
National Staff Coach, NSCAA

Human Kinetics

Library of Congress Cataloging-in-Publication Data

Lennox, James W.
  Soccer skills & drills / James W. Lennox, Janet Rayfield, Bill Steffen.
      p. cm.
   ISBN-13: 978-0-7360-5629-8 (soft cover)
   ISBN-10: 0-7360-5629-7 (soft cover)
   1. Soccer.   I. Rayfield, Janet.   II. Steffen, Bill.   III. National Soccer Coaches Association of America.
IV. Title.   V. Title: Soccer skills and drills.
   GV943.S735 2006
   796.334--dc22

                                        2006011241

ISBN-10: 0-7360-5629-7
ISBN-13: 978-0-7360-5629-8

The Web addresses cited in this text were current as of Feburary 2006, unless otherwise noted.

Acquisitions Editor: Jana Hunter; **Developmental Editor:** Kase Johnstun; **Assistant Editor:** Cory Weber; **Copyeditor:** John Wentworth; **Proofreader:** Erin Cler; **Graphic Designer:** Robert Reuther; **Graphic Artist:** Tara Welsch; **Photo Manager:** Dan Wendt; **Cover Designer:** Keith Blomberg; **Photographer (cover):** © Christof Koepsel/Getty Images; **Photographer (interior):** Sarah Ritz, unless otherwise noted; **Art Manager:** Kareema McLendon; **Illustrator:** Kareema McLendon; **Printer:** Sheridan Books

Human Kinetics books are available at special discounts for bulk purchase. Special editions or book excerpts can also be created to specification. For details, contact the Special Sales Manager at Human Kinetics.

Printed in the United States of America   10 9 8 7 6 5 4 3 2 1

Human Kinetics
Web site: www.HumanKinetics.com

United States: Human Kinetics
P.O. Box 5076
Champaign, IL 61825-5076
800-747-4457
e-mail: humank@hkusa.com

Canada: Human Kinetics
475 Devonshire Road Unit 100
Windsor, ON N8Y 2L5
800-465-7301 (in Canada only)
e-mail: orders@hkcanada.com

Europe: Human Kinetics
107 Bradford Road
Stanningley
Leeds LS28 6AT, United Kingdom
+44 (0) 113 255 5665
e-mail: hk@hkeurope.com

Australia: Human Kinetics
57A Price Avenue
Lower Mitcham, South Australia 5062
08 8277 1555
e-mail: liaw@hkaustralia.com

New Zealand: Human Kinetics
Division of Sports Distributors NZ Ltd.
P.O. Box 300 226 Albany
North Shore City
Auckland
0064 9 448 1207
e-mail: info@humankinetics.co.nz

Contents

Drill Finder

Drill Title	Page #	Individual	Small Group	Team	Tactical	Positional	Opposition	Attack/Defend	Fitness Building
		NUMBER OF PLAYERS			**SKILLS**		**SITUATIONAL**		
CHAPTER 1: DRIBBLING									
Center Circle Dribbling	8			✓		M	W/O	A	
Magnets	10			✓		M	W/O	A	✓
Pairs	10		✓			M	W/O	A	✓
1v2 Dribble	10		✓		Pos, TR, Pen	M	W	B	✓
Four Goal Dribble	11			✓	Pen, Pos, DM, S	M	W	B	✓
Hit the Flag	12	✓			1v1	M	W	B	✓
Winterbottom Duel	13		✓		DM, Pen, TR	M	W	B	✓
Stepover Drill	14	✓				M	W/O	A	
Four Goal Score	15			✓	Pen, Pos, DM	M	W	B	✓
CHAPTER 2: RECEIVING									
Split the Triangle	33		✓			M	W/O	A	✓
Circle Up	33		✓			M	W/O	A	
Horseshoes	34		✓		DM	M	W	B	✓
Numbered Passing	35		✓			M	W/O	A	
Technical Back to Pressure	35		✓			F	W	A	✓
5v5v5	36		✓		Pen, DM	M	W	B	✓
Four Square	36			✓	S, DM, Pos	M	W	B	✓
Three-Zone Possession	37		✓		DM, S, Pos	M	W	A	✓
Back-to-Goal Receiving	38		✓		S, TR, DM	F	W	B	✓
CHAPTER 3: PASSING									
2v2 Serving Drill	49		✓			M	W/O	A	
Short-Short-Long Bending Ball Rhythm	50		✓		DM	M	W	A	✓
Bent Runs, Bent Balls	50		✓			M	W/O	A	
Monkey in the Middle	51			✓	DM, S	M	W	B	✓
End Zone Game	52			✓	Pen, TR	M	W	B	✓
CHAPTER 4: SHOOTING									
Stationary Shooting	60		✓			M	W/O	A	
Finishing Ground Balls	61	✓				M	W/O	A	
Bending the Shot	61	✓				M	W/O	A	
Volley on the Bounce	62	✓				F	W/O	A	
Side-Volley	62	✓				M	W/O	A	
4v4 in Box With Support Players	63		✓		Pen, DM	M	W	B	✓
4v4 With Support Players	63		✓		Pen, DM, S	M	W	B	✓
Distance Shooting	64			✓	Pen, DM, TR	M	W	B	✓

KEY

1v1: One-on-one
DM: Decision making
Pen: Penetration
Pos: Possession
Tr: Transition
S: Spatial awareness

D: Defender
F: Forward
GK: Goalkeeper
M: Multiple
MF: Midfielder

W: With
W/O: Without

A: Attack
D: Defend
B: Both

Drill Title	Page #	NUMBER OF PLAYERS			SKILLS		SITUATIONAL		Fitness Building
		Individual	Small Group	Team	Tactical	Positional	Opposition	Attack/Defend	
CHAPTER 5: HEADING									
Head Juggling	76	✓				M	W/O	B	
Partner Heading	77		✓			M	W/O	A	
Clear or Score	77		✓		DM	M	W/O	A	
2v2 Clear or Score	78		✓		DM	M	W	B	
Center Circle Heading	78			✓		M	W/O	A	
Rotation Heading	79			✓	DM	M	W	A	
Functional Heading	80		✓		DM	M	W/O	A	
CHAPTER 6: TACKLING									
Rock, Paper, Scissors 1v1	91		✓		DM	M	W	D	✓
1v1 to a Line	92	✓			1v1	M	W	B	✓
1v1 With Servers	93	✓			1v1	D	W	B	✓
1v1 to Targets	93	✓			1v1	M	W	B	✓
Mark Your Own Player	94			✓	DM	M	W	D	✓
CHAPTER 7: GOALKEEPING									
Channel Games	109	✓			DM, S	GK	W	D	
Body Line	109	✓				GK	W/O	D	
Cut Off the Angle	110	✓			DM	GK	W	D	✓
Breakaway	110	✓				GK	W	D	✓
CHAPTER 8: APPLYING TECHNIQUES TACTICALLY									
Crossing to Second Six-Yard Box	114		✓		S	M	W/O	A	
Crossing to Near- and Far-Post Spaces	115		✓		DM, S	M	W/O	A	
Crossing to Four Attacking Spaces in Box	115		✓		DM, S	M	W	A	
Crossing With a Neutral Zone	116			✓	DM,S	M	W	B	✓
Central Defender Clearances	118		✓		DM	D	W	D	
Heading Clearances With a Containing Triangle	118		✓		DM, S	M	W	D	
Top-of-Box Heading Clearances	119		✓		DM, S	M	W	D	
Halfway-Line Heading Clearances	120			✓	DM, S	M	W	B	✓
Central Defender Heading to Targets	121		✓		DM, S	D	W	D	
Tracking and Defensive Clearances in Box	122		✓		DM, S	D	W	D	✓

(continued)

KEY

1v1: One-on-one
DM: Decision making
Pen: Penetration
Pos: Possession
Tr: Transition
S: Spatial awareness

D: Defender
F: Forward
GK: Goalkeeper
M: Multiple
MF: Midfielder

W: With
W/O: Without

A: Attack
D: Defend
B: Both

Drill Finder *(continued)*

Drill Title	Page #	NUMBER OF PLAYERS			SKILLS		SITUATIONAL		Fitness Building
		Individual	Small Group	Team	Tactical	Positional	Opposition	Attack/Defend	
Speed Dribbling Through the Thirds	122			✓	DM, Pen	D	W/O	A	✓
Long Passing to Forwards	125		✓			M	W	A	
Changing the Point of Attack	126			✓	Pen, DM, S	M	W	A	✓
Passing to a Checking Striker	128		✓		DM, S	F	W	A	✓
Midfield to Striker to Goal	129			✓	DM, Pen, TR	M	W	B	✓
Breakaway Scoring	130	✓			Pen	F	W	A	
Cutting Off the Defender	130	✓			S, DM	M	W	A	✓
Breakaway Game	131			✓	DM, Pen	M	W	B	✓
CHAPTER 9: DEVELOPING POSITIONAL TACTICS									
Final Pass Game	146		✓		Pen, TR, DM	M	W	B	✓
3v1 to Goal	146		✓		Pen, DM	M	W	A	✓
6 + 1v3	147		✓		S , Pos	M	W	A	✓
2v2 to Corner Goals	148		✓		DM , S	D	W	D	✓
6-Goal Game	149		✓		S, DM, TR	D	W	B	✓
7v7 Two-Zone Game	149			✓	DM, S, TR,	M	W	B	✓

KEY

1v1: One-on-one · DM: Decision making · Pen: Penetration · Pos: Possession · Tr: Transition · S: Spatial awareness
D: Defender · F: Forward · GK: Goalkeeper · M: Multiple · MF: Midfielder
W: With · W/O: Without
A: Attack · D: Defend · B: Both

Introduction

In watching the concluding moments of the men's third-place game in the 2002 World Cup between South Korea and Turkey, one had the sense that great soccer, more than any other sport, has the ability to lift us to the highest plane of human emotional experience. The postgame celebrations, in which both teams linked arms and conducted a lap of honor in front of 75,000 fans, lingers in memory as one of the great moments in sport history.

The game itself pulsated from one end of the field to the other with spellbinding speed and superb technical mastery. The defeated South Koreans sobbed at the final whistle, only to be swept up by the jubilant Turks, who clasped their hands and began a joint tribute to the fans. This gesture between countries with almost nothing in common aside from their love of the game symbolized the power and beauty of soccer.

Pelé, arguably the greatest soccer player ever, labeled the sport, "The Beautiful Game." In doing so he forever set a standard for which we must continually strive. There is simply no other game that can bind and enthrall the people of the globe together in a common language and purpose. There is no other sport to which rich and poor have such equal access, where the only equipment needed is a ball. From the streets of Glasgow, to the barrios of Brazil, to the sandy desert of Egypt, soccer is all about a ball—and learning to master it.

THE FIRST SOCCER SKILL

The fascination with the ball begins with a child's first steps and continues in the over-50 and over-60 age-group leagues that dot our landscape. Long before other people become the opposition, the ball itself is the opponent, to be mastered and tamed—because "if you don't control the ball, the ball will control you." Although everyone has his or her own interpretation of exactly what constitutes beautiful soccer, most commentators agree that the game is only beautiful when played by players with a high level of ball mastery.

The lawmakers of the game, from very early on, recognized that the entertainment value of soccer contributed to its vast appeal. Those who first crafted the rules, conscious of soccer as an aesthetic commodity, cautioned referees against "continuous whistling for trifling infringements" because this spoiled the enjoyment of players and spectators. But officials aren't responsible for the technical incompetence of players on the field. And soccer is a complete mess when played by players who cannot control, pass, or dribble the ball with proficiency.

Technical mastery is highly prized, especially when coupled with agility, speed, and savvy. We admire the player whose technical ability has a direct impact on the game. It is the application of techniques at just the right time and place that constitutes skill. And it is skill that we all admire—not a bag of party tricks performed in isolated areas of the field where they have no impact on the game.

NEVER TOO EARLY TO START

A study in England many years ago tracked the technical development of players who were under consideration for entry into the Football Association's player-development program at Lilleshall, the national training center. The study concluded that once past the age of 14 it is very difficult for players to correct poor mechanical technique—largely because of the extraordinary strength of habit development between the ages of 6 and 14, considered "the golden years of learning."

The need to develop good soccer habits early on was reinforced by another study conducted by the Scottish Football Association. The results revealed that many of their top international players possessed a set of four common characteristics:

- Most came from areas with strong youth clubs and leagues.
- One or both parents had an athletic background.
- They seized an opportunity to develop, such as being recognized by a talent scout or getting a chance to play when a teammate was injured.
- Someone significant in their life (e.g., parent, relative, coach, trainer) positively influenced their interest and growth in the game.

Aimes Jacquet, manager of the great French World Cup champions of 1998 said, "The trainer is the most important person in football." Trainers, or coaches, directly affect the way players are developed and, consequently, the way the game is played. They decide a player's position on the field, how much playing time the player gets, and whether to recommend a player for a higher level or cut the player from the squad. Most important, the coach can be the most powerful force in the life of a young person who is deciding to make a full commitment to the game or pursue other avenues. Thus, instruction and inspiration are the two main tasks of a coach today.

This book has been written for both players and those who coach and train them. The material that follows, covering soccer techniques and their effective use in competition, must be learned at some point. And, as pointed out in the study cited previously, the earlier the skills of the sport are learned, developed, and mastered, the better.

FOUR STAGES OF SKILL MASTERY

Andy Roxburgh, former Scottish national team coach and current technical director of the Union of European Football Association (UEFA), described skill acquisition as occurring in four stages:

1. Unconscious Incompetence

Initially, the individual performs a skill incorrectly and does not realize it. Repetition of incorrect technique eventually becomes so ingrained that it is almost impossible to correct. The flaw might be rudimentary or quite complex. This is where a skilled trainer is needed. A trainer must have the experience and information to recognize the playing fault and the demonstration ability to show the player how the technique is properly done.

2. Conscious Incompetence

Once aware of a flaw, a player can respond in one of four ways:

- Accept constructive criticism and engage in activities that address the problem and that successfully change the performance of the skill
- Accept constructive criticism but not be able to address the problem because of physical inability
- Accept constructive criticism but fail to address the problem because of a lack of desire
- Reject the constructive criticism

Obviously, the first outcome listed is the preferred one.

3. Conscious Competence

The difficulty of changing a habit should not be underestimated. For many athletes, mechanical skills performed repetitively continue to feel awkward for quite some time. The conscious effort to do something differently meets with a great deal of physical resistance because the body is being forced into new patterns of movement. At this stage, the player must still think before executing.

4. Unconscious Competence

Somebody once said, "First you make your habits, then your habits make you." A habit can be described as an unconscious performance of an acquired physical skill. This is the goal of technical training—to make the correct movements and their timing so automatic that the player responds instinctively and correctly in appropriate situations.

Soccer skill mastery involves doing the right thing, at the right time, in the right part of the field, and without thinking about it. Soccer players will work in vain on the tactical aspects of soccer until they no longer have to look at the ball continuously while dribbling, can elude a defender when necessary, and can pass or shoot effectively when the opportunity arises. Such habits are acquired through a complex interaction of modeling (seeing how something is done), practice (repetition of correct skills against and with other good players), and motivation (being in an environment where good soccer skills are valued).

Study, practice, and value the techniques presented in this book. Soccer is indeed a beautiful game when played with a skill and flair that both astonish and inspire.

Key to Diagrams

A — Attacker

D — Defender

GK — Goalkeeper

Cr — Crosser

S — Server

F — Forward

MF — Midfielder

B — Back

X — Player

C — Coach

Cone

Flag

Soccer ball

- - - → Path of ball

——→ Path of player

∿∿∿→ Path of player dribbling the ball

Dribbling

Diego Maradona's electrifying dribble to score Argentina's second goal against England in the 1986 World Cup quarterfinal was one of the most exciting moments in soccer history. Receiving the ball close to the halfway line, Maradona exploded through England's defense and passed defender after defender before rolling the ball behind a prone and helpless Peter Shilton. Maradona's combination of dribbling skill, speed, and agility froze a few moments in time never to be forgotten among soccer fans.

Nothing sets apart the skillful soccer player more than the ability to dribble. When we think of the greatest players, what do we remember about them? Sir Stanley Matthews, Pelé, Diego Maradona, Mia Hamn, Helga Riise—all of these players exhibited the ability to dribble in all interpretations of the skill. Their improvisational dribbling was the singular feature that riveted our attention.

Today, we can sense the crowd's anticipation when Ronaldinho, young Cristiano Ronaldo, or Marta receives the ball. What is it about Freddy Adu that we all go to see? Each of these young, gifted players can beat opponents on the dribble, keep possession in the tightest of spaces, and make a foot (30 cm) of space from which to pass, cross, or shoot. When these players attack and beat defenders, you hear announcers use such words as "explosive," "penetrating," and "elusive," and these qualities are exactly what make these players so special.

Those rare players with outstanding individual technique on the ball are typically the ones we judge as the best and most exciting players on the field. A combination of natural talent, intense soccer environment, and proper training is the triumvirate that forges such technical expertise. Players genetically endowed with a high percentage of fast-twitch muscle fibers and an explosive perceptual processing ability often need only to grow up in an intense soccer environment to become adept players on the ball. Even players who are not genetically gifted, however, can attain excellent skills on the ball if they're willing to practice dribbling skills on their own and play in as many quality games as they can find.

Coaches working with players in their preteen years should devote a major portion of their training to dribbling technique. The preteen years, especially, are the years of individual technique and the 1v1 duel. New neuromuscular patterns are more easily imprinted and retained during these years. The players' enthusiasm and response to instruction should be at a zenith. As players reach the midteen years, dribbling training tends to become more functional, or position oriented, and involves less time in training sessions. With midteen or older players, dribbling for the outside back might focus on running the ball, whereas dribbling training for a forward is more of a combination of screening, escape moves, and feints to beat defenders.

General technical training for dribbling is best done in a large, confined space with a ball for each player. Constant correct repetition of technique is required to improve a skill, and giving each player a ball allows everyone to execute repeated trials of each technique or subtechnique. Technical training for dribbling proceeds from general training, which is usually done in a confined space and is nondirectional (such as activities done in a circle), to directional activities that might incorporate cones, flags, and small-sided games (e.g., 1v2) using smaller goals.

Dribbling can be categorized into three types: dribbling to beat an opponent, dribbling to maintain possession, and speed dribbling (running with the ball to elude a defender or to attack a space).

DRIBBLING TO BEAT AN OPPONENT

The tactical situation at hand determines how a player will utilize dribbling. A flank player who receives the ball and is facing an isolated defender will attack the defender's front leg (figure 1.1a) and play the ball into the space behind the defender (figure 1.1b). The player will then explode into the space behind the defender to

a   b

Figure 1.1 (a) Player attacks defender's front leg, and (b) plays ball into space behind defender.

be first to the ball. A different tactical scenario may find a forward receiving the ball under immediate pressure from one or more defenders and having no supporting teammates; in this case, the forward must dribble to keep possession until support arrives (figure 1.2). An outside back who is played out of the back third must run the ball vertically at speed to explode through the middle third.

Figure 1.2 Player receives ball under immediate pressure and must dribble until help arrives.

Dribbling to beat an opponent typically occurs in the middle, and most often in the attacking third of the field. In the middle third, attackers often have the opportunity to run at defenders because there is more space between and behind defenders. The attacking midfield player is usually one of the best dribblers on the team and will look to attack opponent midfield players. When these frontal dribbles are successful, the central midfield player is now unpressured, has a maximum cone of vision of the field, and can play the ball forward through any angle. The dribbler with good passing range is even more effective because all of his or her teammates are within technical range. Likewise, flank attackers, whether midfield players or outside backs, often find space available as they attack up the flanks.

In the final third, dribbling to beat an opponent is essential, because whenever a player has dribbled a defender, he or she might be able to deliver a final pass (a pass from which a shot will ensue) or shoot. Players who are successful at dribbling and beating defenders on the flank are able to hit crosses into the box. In today's sophisticated defensive structures, most goals are created by good crosses from the flank.

DRIBBLING TO MAINTAIN POSSESSION

Dribbling to maintain possession and escape is the mark of a maturing soccer player. Very young or inexperienced players don't recognize the importance of being able to keep possession of the ball for their team. Too often they will try to beat every opponent by dribbling, turn the ball into a defender, or attempt to pass the ball into impossible angles. In each of these cases possession of the ball is lost.

As players gain experience, they recognize that a team that can maintain possession can control a game and prepare attacks that result in effective penetration to achieve crosses, passes, and shots that threaten the opponent's goal.

Midfield players and forwards, especially, must be able to hold the ball under pressure of opponents so that teammates have time to take up good supporting positions. Teams today often play with packed midfield defensive schemes to try to stop attacks before they get organized. This means that players who can maintain possession and escape from double-team tactics are invaluable. Forwards are often asked to play in advanced positions without a lot of supporting players nearby. When teams prepare attacks from deep positions, forwards often receive a long ball played up to them and must maintain possession until supporting teammates can arrive to help.

Players who play on the flank must be skilled at keeping the ball and escaping. Unlike central players, flank midfielders and outside backs must play close to the touchline, and defenders always try to pin these wide players against the touchline. Double teaming on the flank is an effective defensive tactic, with two defenders pressing the attacker against the touchline; in such a case, if the attacker is good at holding and escaping, his or her team can continue the attack.

In many cases, and especially for younger players, extra time is needed to work on maintaining possession and escaping. In general, coaches will want to spend as much time as possible on dribbling skills, and the critical subtechnique of maintaining possession is as important to stress as any other.

While working on maintaining possession and escaping, coaches should frequently remind players how using different foot surfaces and foot angles alters what they can do with the ball. When they want to run the ball straight ahead, they should push their toe down and strike the ball by pushing it with the instep or outside of the foot (figure 1.3) Coaches might say, "Toe down to run the ball." When players want to move the ball laterally, they should pull the toe up to turn the ball laterally, especially when spinning with the ball in possession (figure 1.4). Coaches might say, "Toe up to move the ball laterally in a tight situation." (Later we explain how the ball can be *chopped* with the instep to change direction.)

While practicing maintaining possession, as players get close to each other, they should raise the toe and escape, or spin away. If a long space is available, players should push the ball long, explode into the space to reach the ball, and begin running it with the instep. Each time they encounter other players, they should again escape by raising the toe and spinning in a new direction.

Again, coaches should work on dribbling as much as time allows, particularly for younger players, and should be as specific as possible with their coaching points. They should remind players to change speed and direction, run the ball, or escape, focusing on one concept per drill or exercise. If the focus is on escape and spinning out, coaches should remind players to keep their toes up; they should also explain the necessity of bending at the knees and hips to achieve a low center of gravity so they can turn quickly and remain stable if contact occurs. Players should be reminded to hold their arms out and up a bit for balance and to ward off opponents.

Figure 1.3 Push toe down to strike ball with instep or outside of the foot.

Figure 1.4 Pull toe up to turn ball laterally.

As players practice maintaining possession and escaping, coaches will likely also want to observe how they change speed and run the ball, but at this point coaching points should be restricted to the one critical area of keeping possession and escaping.

SPEED DRIBBLING

Speed dribbling is a specialized form of dribbling that allows players to run the ball vertically while in possession. Situations occur when players have the ball at their feet and lots of space ahead to move into. Players always have the choice of passing the ball forward, but teammates are not always open, so sometimes the best decision is to run the ball forward at speed. The purpose of speed dribbling is always to try to gain territory before the defense can organize behind the ball.

The best example of speed dribbling in modern soccer occurs during counter-attacks. Whether a ball is played up to a forward who then tries to outrace the retreating defense or a midfield player breaks out of the back third and runs the ball through the middle third, the faster these players can run the ball, the less time defenders have to get back behind the ball and organize their collective defending action.

On a team that features outstanding attacking fullbacks, the ability of these players to run the ball through the middle third once they have been played out of the back third is essential to unbalancing opposing defenders.

Finally, flank midfielders must be able to speed dribble, especially when they are dribbling past an opponent out wide. If they can run the ball at speed in this situation, they might get into position to shoot, pass to teammates, or get in crosses before the next defender can get wide to pressure them.

Each of these categories of dribbling is different, and coaches must know when each type should be applied; training should be designed to prepare players to execute the correct dribbling technique for each kind of tactical situation. Emphasize that dribbling is part of a technical process. Before dribbling, a player must be able to receive a ball efficiently in preparation for dribbling, and once dribbling is concluded, the player must be able to shoot or pass effectively.

For very young players, preparation for explosive dribbling begins with activities that involve explosive starts, stops, and changes of direction. Dribbling requires the ability to twist, turn, and fake one way and then go the other. Players who are keeping possession must perform these movements to unbalance a defender in one direction so they can turn in the opposite direction to escape. Dribblers must be able to plant a foot, dip a shoulder, and then explosively push off in the other direction. Players might receive a pass that they can push ahead to accelerate into a speed dribble. Activities that mimic these movements include tag games, relay races (run backward, hop on one foot, and so on), and soccer ball gymnastics. For older players, ballistic resistance training and plyometrics may be added.

PERFORMING FEINTS

A basic skill acquired early by most soccer players is the use of the feint. Most often, a feint is used when a player wants to dribble past an opponent. Some feints are patterned movements that can be practiced to deceive and unbalance defenders. Coaches should teach preteen players the mechanics of various kinds of feints as well as their tactical applications. Young players need to learn when and why one feint works better than another in a particular situation. For instance, a feint to escape pressure is likely different from a feint to beat an opponent in a frontal dribble. Demonstrate each kind of feint and explain when to use them most effectively. During drills or games, interrupt play for coaching points to explain why a particular feint worked well or why a different feint would have worked better.

When explaining, the coach will need to clearly demonstrate the feint's mechanics. Ask players to mimic the movement, first in slow motion to make sure they can perform the mechanics correctly. The coach must be patient and sensitive to players' needs during the learning phase. Once players can execute the feint correctly at a slow speed, they then try to do it faster. Some players will need more time than others to get the movement pattern down, and the coach will need to spend more time with these players.

A typical patterned movement or feint to escape pressure is to play the ball behind the standing leg. Facing an opponent, the player steps beyond the ball with one leg and then pulls the ball behind that standing leg with the inside of the other foot (figure 1.5).

A classic feint to defeat a defender in a fontal dribble is the stepover. With the ball in front of the body, the right foot steps diagonally over the ball and lands on the ground beyond and to the right of the ball. The right shoulder is dipped to the right as the stepover is executed. As the right leg plants and flexes, the ball is pushed hard diagonally forward and left of the defender with the left foot (figure 1.6). Once the mechanics of the stepover are patterned, the player may do a double stepover, in which the right foot steps over the ball first, then the left, followed by the right foot pushing the ball beyond the defender.

During practice games the coach can stop players to explain how a low center of gravity and wider base of support allow for quick changes of direction. Likewise, to stop quickly, a player must lower the center of gravity and widen the base of support. Explosive starts require that joints at the ankle, knee, and hip are flexed, or loaded, prior to extension.

Figure 1.5 Step over ball and pull it behind forward leg with instep or inside of foot.

Figure 1.6 Step over ball diagonally to the right, drop shoulder, and push left of the defender.

DRIBBLING DRILLS

Dribbling is the singular feature that identifies a mature, experienced player. While we all want to watch players whose serpentine dribbles leave defenders strewn behind them, only a select few are anointed with such gifts. Most players need a complete repertoire of dribbling skills and should know when to implement these skills in various tactical situations. In particular, today's player should be able to maintain possession of the ball, escape, or make a half-yard (.46 m) of space to pass the ball. Defending, both individually and collectively, is increasingly more organized to pressure the attacking team and win the ball back as quickly as possible. To keep the ball, players must be able to combat high-pressure defending with flawless dribbling skills.

Center Circle Dribbling

Purpose: To practice the technical points of dribbling

Procedure: Figure 1.7a shows 16 players in the center circle. Ten cones are placed around the center circle, 20 yards (18.2 m) outside the circle. Players are asked to dribble in the center circle while keeping possession of their ball and not running into teammates.

Coaching Points: Emphasize the technical points of dribbling. Give general instructions that apply to all dribbling techniques.

Variation 1: At the coach's command of "Cones!" players leave the circle and sprint with their ball to the cones, circle a cone, and run the ball at speed back to the circle (figure 1.7b). The coach observes the players' technique of running the ball.

The first push should be a long one because a long push allows the player to run faster between touches. When a player has a lot of space in front or when breaking away from an opponent, the first touch should be 10 or more feet. As he or she approaches the cone, the touches will be closer together for control in preparation for rounding the cone.

Variation 2: Once back in the circle, players continue to dribble. On the command "Spin!" each player stops and, with toe up, spins in a 360-degree circle while keeping the ball tight to the body. Players spin using the inside of the foot in one direction and the outside of the foot in the other.

Variation 3: Add the game "Knockout" (figure 1.7c). Players dribble randomly outside the circle, and on command they must cross through the center circle to the farthest point of the other side. As players cross, they attempt to knock a teammate's ball out of the circle.

The variations of this drill are general dribbling warm-up exercises to give the coach more information for assessment purposes. In variation 1, the coach can train and assess the players' ability to run the ball. In variations 2 and 3, the coach can observe how well players escape or beat an opponent. By alternating commands and stopping to make coaching points, coaches can keep these drills interesting and challenging.

With players all practicing the same feint in the center circle, the coach is close enough to observe the performance of each player and can efficiently stop the exercise to make corrections or emphasize coaching points.

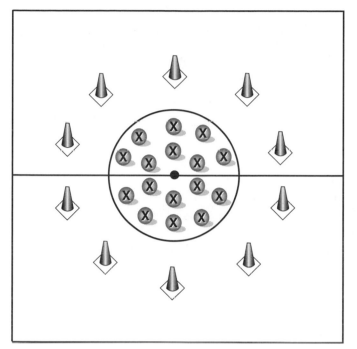

Figure 1.7a Center Circle Dribbling.

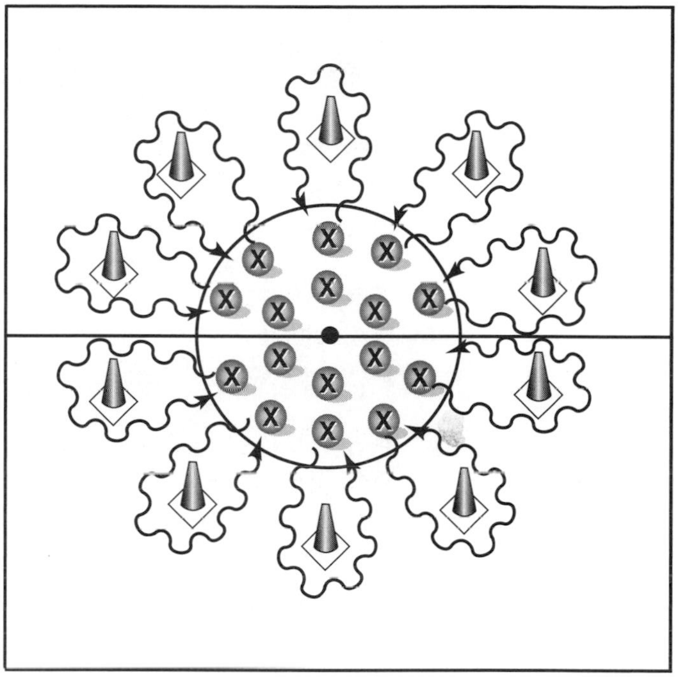

Figure 1.7b Center Circle Dribbling, variation 1.

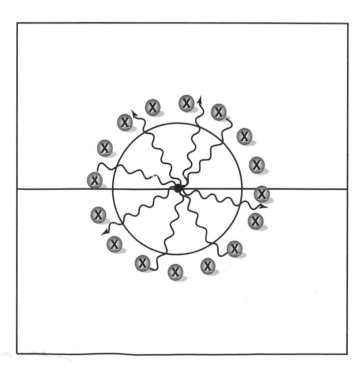

Figure 1.7c Center Circle Dribbling, variation 3.

Magnets

Purpose: To practice keeping possession and escaping

Procedure: The coach creates a mental image for players by describing a game that works similarly to the repulsion effect of magnets. When like poles of two magnets approach each other, they repel and push each other away. Place players in a circle and ask them to begin dribbling; when a dribbler approaches another player, they repel each other and dribble in opposite directions.

Coaching Points: Players must keep the ball close to their feet, flex their knees when changing directions, and accelerate into a new direction.

Pairs

Purpose: To escape defensive pressure in game time situations

Procedure: In a circle, players form pairs with one ball. While one player is in possession, the other puts a hand on the back of the player in possession. The objective is for the players in possession to twist and turn and make their partner's hand come off their back.

Coaching Points: Players must look up under their eyebrows to have vision of where they want to go, change speed and direction, and accelerate into a new direction.

Variation: Players are in pairs, each player holds a pinnie in one hand. The two battle in a 1v1 duel to see who can keep possession longer. They can switch the hand in which they hold the pinnie, but they can't let it go.

1v2 Dribble

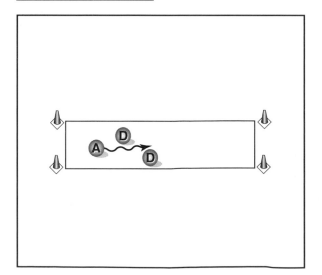

Purpose: To keep possession under pressure of two defenders; to beat and score against two defenders

Procedure: Three players play in an area 10 to 12 yards (9.1-10.9 m) long by 18 to 25 yards (16.4-22.8 m) wide. An attacker plays 1v2 and tries to dribble past the two defenders to score a goal between the cones (figure 1.8). If a defender wins the ball, he or she plays 1v2 to attack the other goal. The exercise is always 1v2, with the player winning the ball going to the opposite goal.

Figure 1.8 1v2 Dribble.

Four Goal Dribble

Purpose: To progress to more specific training for possession and escaping

Procedure: Figure 1.9a shows a four-goal exercise in an area 20 yards (18.2 m) by 30 yards (27.4 m). Cones mark four goals (3 to 4 feet [.9-1.2 m] wide), two each along the long sides. Two player pairs are inside, and two pairs wait along each sideline. On the coach's signal, two 1v1 duels occur. The objective is for the attacker (A) to dribble past the defender (D) and score at either goal. The attacker keeps the ball until the other player dispossesses him or her, and then that player tries to score. When someone scores, they can't score again into the same goal. There are two 1v1s going on at the same time. After 1 minute, the coach signals to stop, and now the two sets of players waiting on the sidelines go in to duel while the first two pairs rest.

Coaching Points: Fitness levels determine how many repetitions to perform. Setting up two fields will involve 16 players.

Variation: Figure 1.9b shows a variation of figure 1.9a. One player stands behind each goal. When one of the players dueling in the game dribbles through the cones to score, the player behind the goal gets the ball and goes inside to continue the 1v1 duel, while the player who just scored rests.

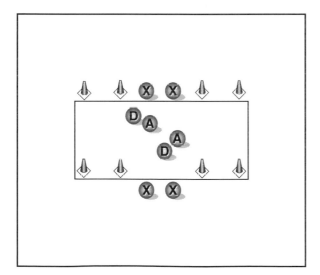

Figure 1.9a Four Goal Dribble.

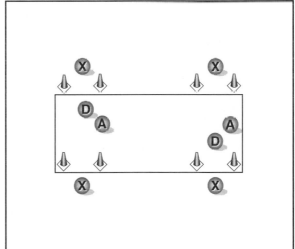

Figure 1.9b Four Goal Dribble, variation.

Hit the Flag

Purpose: To practice escaping and running the ball

Procedure: In figure 1.10 players are in pairs with one ball per pair. Flags are placed on the field, as shown. The objective is for the attacker to hit the flag by passing the ball toward it. Because many shots miss the flag, both players race to gain possession of the ball. The player who arrives at the ball first is usually closely followed by the opponent and thus will have to screen the ball from the opponent. Here the subtechnique of keeping possession and escape is repeatedly practiced. Because it's difficult to hit such a small target, the player in possession runs the ball at speed to try to get closer to the flag before shooting. Here the subtechnique of running the ball is practiced. The work–rest ratio for the drill is one minute of competition, then one minute of rest. The number of repetitions should be set according to the fitness level of the players.

Coaching Points: While players participate in Hit the Flag, the coach has many opportunities to stop and make suggestions or corrections. The coach may stop the entire group to make an overall point, such as when screening the ball, the player should play the ball with the far foot, be sideways to the opponent, and use the arm as a bar to increase the distance between the opponent and the ball.

The coach may also choose to stop only one pair to make a suggestion, such as when an opponent is partially beaten, push the ball diagonally across the opponent's line of recovery. Now the opponent will be impeded by the dribbler's body.

When dribbling, the feet should stay close to the ground as they move. Feet lifted higher to perform turns or feints slows the speed of movement and gives opponents time to react.

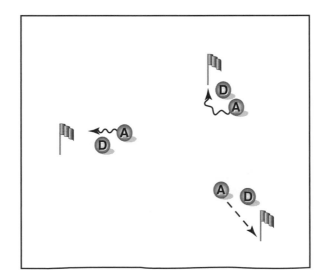

Figure 1.10 Hit the Flag.

Winterbottom Duel

Purpose: To perform a classic exercise for dribbling and the 1v1 duel

Procedure: Two players stand 30 yards (27.4 m) apart (figure 1.11a), each with legs apart to represent a goal. Each player has an extra ball so that the exercise never stops. A second pair of players are positioned between the pair who are functioning as goals. The objective of the exercise is for the inside players to engage in a 1v1 duel, with the player in possession trying to beat the opponent and pass or dribble the ball through the open legs of either goal. This is a minigame with each player attacking in one direction. If the opponent wins the ball, he or she attacks the opposite goal. If a player shoots and misses the goal, the player who was acting as the goal kicks the extra ball in the air for the 1v1 players to battle for possession.

Coaching Points: Named for Walter Winterbottom, the famous and revered English director of coaching during the 1950s, the Winterbottom Duel has been used around the world for 50 years. The drill is done for 45 to 60 seconds. After 60 seconds, the coach stops the drill, at which point the dueling pair become the goals and the goals come inside to play 1v1. The number of repetitions is based on the fitness level of the players.

Variation: Figure 1.11b shows the modified Winterbottom. The organization and the objective are the same. Now, though, if the attacker beats the defender, the attacker can pass the ball to the goal, and—rather than letting the ball go through his or her legs—the goal wall passes back to the attacker, and the attacker attacks the opposite goal.

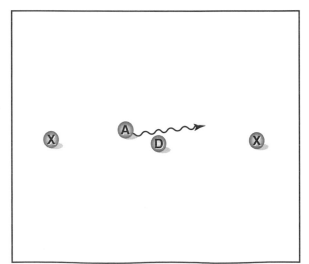

Figure 1.11a Winterbottom Duel.

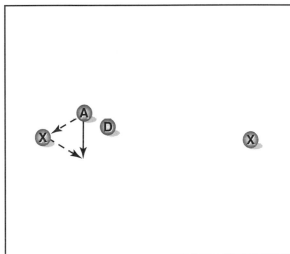

Figure 1.11b Winterbottom Duel, variation.

Stepover Drill

Purpose: To tactically apply feint skills developed in a circle

Procedure: Defenders stand 4 to 5 yards (3.6-4.5 m) out from the box (figure 1.12a). Attackers dribble toward their respective defenders and execute a stepover or double stepover to unbalance the defender. After feinting, the attacker then shoots. Defenders are told to stand still and lean with the fake, but they're not to try to win the ball. Attackers may use the stepover to either side of the defender.

Variation: Again, attackers have two defenders to beat with the stepover. The variation is to allow the standing defenders to move by stepping toward the dribbler with one leg (figure 1.12b). Only one leg may be moved, and the defender must keep the other leg planted and stationary. This variation provides a game-related phase in which the dribbler can practice the stepover technique under increased (but not full) pressure from a defender.

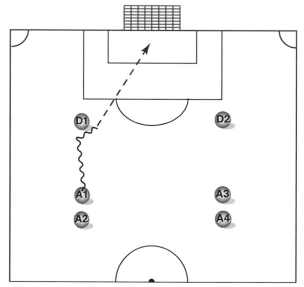

Figure 1.12a   Stepover Drill.

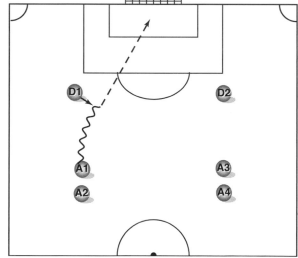

Figure 1.12b   Stepover Drill, variation.

GAMES

All training sessions should end with a real game that lasts from 20 to 30 minutes. The game need not be 11v11—it could be 7v7, 9v9, or something else—as long as play occurs on an appropriate sized field for the number of players participating. Once the game is under way, the coach should coach only during the first 10 to 15 minutes, focusing on the skills being stressed for the day. After 10 to 15 minutes, the coach should step off the field and let the players play the remaining time with no interference. The players need to play uninterrupted to see if they can incorporate the focus of the training session. The play at this point should resemble a game with the coach only observing as he or she would during the full game.

Four Goal Score

Purpose: To practice the skills emphasized in the training session

Procedure: If the emphasis for the session is dribbling, a lead-in exercise before the game may be done (figure 1.13). On a field 60 yards (54.8 m) long by 44 yards (40.2 m) wide, play 6v6 plus goalkeepers, and use full-sized goals. Additionally, place four small goals at the edge of the middle and final thirds of the field, two at each end. Scoring is as usual to the full goal, but a team can also score by dribbling through the small goals.

Coaching Points: The coach should encourage aggressive dribbling whenever the tactical situation dictates.

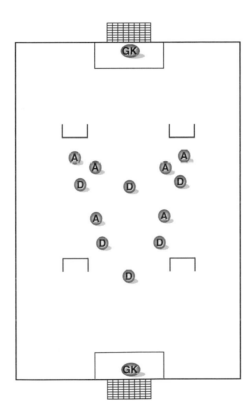

Figure 1.13 Four Goal Score.

Receiving

There's much more to receiving than just trapping the ball. Receiving involves not only gaining control of a moving ball but also being prepared to use the ball in performing a subsequent skill or tactic quickly and effectively. The true skill of receiving involves anticipating what's about to transpire on the field so that the player's first touch of the ball, which is so critical, prepares him or her optimally for the next action. In this regard, the first touch is really a preparation touch that allows the player to set up the action to be executed next. As we tell our players, it's one thing to get control of the ball and another to do something positive with it.

In this chapter we'll discuss both the basics of receiving—gaining control of the ball and bringing it close to the body—and the more highly skilled receiving techniques that permit a player to quickly and effectively employ skills and tactics immediately after the reception.

RECEIVING GROUND BALLS

Balls played on the ground can be received with any of the three main surfaces of the foot: inside, outside, or instep. Which part of the foot is used depends on the angle of the incoming ball and the action the player wants to take immediately after receiving it. A defender pressuring you as you receive the ball with your back to the goal might necessitate receiving the ball with the outside of the foot to keep your body between the defender and the ball. The inside of the foot is very effective in receiving a ball when you're facing your attacking direction; you open your hips, receive the ball across your body, and have the greatest vision of the options for passing or dribbling. You might choose to use the instep to receive a ball when your intent is to take the space on the dribble.

Many coaches emphasize the need to cushion the ball, or take the pace off it, so that the ball remains close and a player can maintain possession. Although cushioning can be critical and is a great starting point for young players, the ultimate goal is to control the pace of the incoming ball and redirect it in the desired direction. The essential element is that the first touch prepares the player for the *next* action to be performed. For example, say a player receives a short pass from a nearby player, while 45 yards (41 m) away a teammate starts to make a run down the line for a ball to be served into the space behind the defense. The player receiving the pass wants to receive with a touch in the direction that opens up a passing lane to the running teammate. If pressure is coming, that touch should be taken away from the oncoming pressure. The distance of the touch should be far enough that the player can take a step into the ball and strike a long pass to the running teammate. In contrast, a player receiving a pass under tight pressure must take a touch away from pressure while keeping the touch close so that the pressuring defender can't step in and tackle the ball away. To solve the tight pressure, the receiving player is most likely looking to make a short pass, and a shorter touch will allow that short pass to be made. As mentioned previously, a player receiving the ball with the intent to dribble forward into open space can effectively use the instep surface of the foot. The attacking player wants to make the first touch as long as possible so that he or she can sprint forward without having to touch the ball as often. This is much quicker and more effective than trapping the ball and then starting to run with it.

In most situations an active first touch, one in which the player and the ball move together, is a much more important and applicable skill than simply stopping a ball with the feet. Regardless of the surface, body position and muscle control are the keys to receiving. The receiver must be able to stabilize the body and even absorb contact from an opponent while simultaneously relaxing the leg that will receive the ball in order to control the pace of the incoming pass. A low and balanced stance, centered over the plant leg (the leg that remains on the ground when a player is receiving a ball with the other foot), allows the receiver not only to control the pace of the incoming pass but also to move with the ball, as the first touch is played with the intent to pass long to a teammate, to take space, to beat an opponent, or to shoot on goal (figure 2.1).

Inside of the Foot

As mentioned before, the inside of the foot is most often used to receive a ball and play in the direction the player is currently facing or to play across the body as the player looks to switch the point of attack to the opposite side of the field. The inside of the foot is often the proper surface when the player has time and space to receive the ball and is facing the direction in which his or her team is attacking.

When receiving with the inside of the foot, the ankle is flexed (toe up) to provide a large surface area with which to contact the ball (figure 2.2). The leg should be rotated so that the inside of the foot is perpendicular to the direction the player wishes to play the ball. The plant leg should be bent to allow the player to move with the ball, making the touch active. An active touch, one which takes the player away from the spot he or she receives the ball, allows a player to control the ball and avoid oncoming pressure.

The degree to which a player cushions the ball on impact depends on the pace of the incoming pass and the desired length of the first touch. The point of contact on the ball should be just above the horizontal middle to ensure that the ball remains on the ground and is not "popped up," creating the necessity for additional touches.

Outside of the Foot

The same low and balanced stance used when receiving with the inside of the foot is used with the outside of the foot as well. The outside of the foot is an excellent option when receiving the ball under the pressure of an opponent because it allows a player to keep a greater distance between the ball and the opponent. By positioning the body sideways on to the defender and receiving with the outside of the foot, the player has the width of his or her

Figure 2.1 Correct body position for active first touch.

Figure 2.2 Receiving with the inside of the foot.

body between the pressuring defender and the ball. Proper foot position normally has the toe slightly pointed downward and inward (figure 2.3). This creates a flat surface with the outside portion of the instep that contacts the top half of the ball, again keeping the ball on the ground for ease of service, a shot, or dribbling.

The instep is used very similarly to the outside of the foot when controlling a ball on the ground but is used to create a more penetrating (as opposed to lateral) first touch (figure 2.4). When making an active first touch with the inside or outside of the foot, the attacking player is usually moving away from pressure in a lateral direction—moving to the right or left of the defender to create an opening to pass, shoot, or even to dribble into. With the instep, the object is usually to penetrate forward into an open space. The instep is the proper surface for this because it allows the player to receive the ball without changing the natural running motion. Most athletes run with their toes pointed forward, and using the instep allows a natural stride, which means the player penetrates faster into the open space. Note that slightly pigeon-toed athletes (and there are many such players with many talents in the sport of soccer) can use the outside of their foot and accomplish the same objective.

Figure 2.3 Creating a flat surface for receiving the ball with the outside of the foot.

Figure 2.4 Receiving with the instep.

RECEIVING AIR BALLS

The objective when receiving a ball out of the air is to get the ball to the ground under control so it can be played as soon as possible. For higher skilled players, the objective might be to put the ball in a position to volley (as in a shot or clearance) or to serve the ball out of the air.

The first and often overlooked element of receiving balls out of the air is to choose a surface with which to receive the ball. Many players, especially young players, just get their body behind the ball and allow it to hit them anywhere (such as the abdomen or the shin), hoping that the ball will settle to their feet.

So, choosing the best receiving surface and then positioning that surface behind the ball is an important first step of the reception process. As is true of foot position in receiving ground balls, the contacting surface for receiving air balls should be perpendicular to the direction the player wishes to take the ball with the first touch. For balls in the air, an active first touch is much more challenging. Players should look to master getting the ball out of the air and to the ground as quickly as possible and then advance to taking balls out of the air with an active touch.

Receiving With the Chest

The chest can be a great surface to settle flighted or driven balls. A flighted ball generally has a lot of loft and less pace than a driven ball; typically, it has some backspin and thus will most likely be coming downward toward the chest. A driven ball might have a much lower trajectory and will often be at or below chest height. Depending on the situation, the angle of the chest on contact will vary. Any time the ball is slightly below chest height, the angle of the chest can point downward as the ball is received, redirecting the ball immediately to the ground. The chest must be positioned behind the ball, and the upper body must be relaxed to take as much momentum off the ball as possible (figure 2.5a). The greater the pace of the ball, the more difficult it will be to redirect the ball to the ground at a pace that can be easily played. As the ball contacts the chest, the player bends slightly at the waist, angling the chest over the ball so that the ball is directed downward (figure 2.5b).

a   b

Figure 2.5 (a) Relax the upper body and position the chest behind the ball, then (b) bend slightly at the waist to project the ball downward.

Receiving with the chest leaves the ball exposed, so therefore players normally receive with the chest when they are not under great pressure. In such cases, they'll have the opportunity to make a second touch to prepare the ball for a shot or service. It is the quickness, however, that makes this kind of touch advantageous. For example, a driven clearance out of the back toward a defensive midfielder who has some time and space might be chested down to his or her feet so he or she can take a touch and then serve the ball back into the box. Chesting the ball immediately downward is quicker than the more lofted touch and thus allows for the service to be made before the onrushing defense can apply pressure.

A ball coming with greater pace or coming from above the chest height can be settled by angling the chest more upward, presenting something like a tabletop surface to contact the ball. In such a reception, the upper body must be relaxed so that the momentum of the ball is absorbed by the upper body; the ball is then allowed to drop to the feet of the receiving player or volleyed out of the air. Bent knees and an arched back provide the cushioning effect necessary to take pace off the ball. The angle of the chest is slightly upward and directly behind the ball (figure 2.6a), but as the body relaxes at the moment of contact, the ball rests momentarily on the chest (figure 2.6b). To get the ball to the ground, a second touch (usually and most effectively with the instep) is required, and this touch can and should be active when the situation dictates (figure 2.6c).

a   b   c

Figure 2.6 (a) Knees are bent and back is arched backward. (b) Body relaxes at moment of impact and ball rests momentarily on the chest. (c) A second touch settles the ball to the ground.

With just one touch, highly-skilled players can redirect the ball's course in the direction they wish by altering the angle of the chest when receiving the ball. These players are also able to take a second touch out of the air directly as a volley, which can then become either a serve to a teammate or a shot (figure 2.7, a-d). For example, say a striker at the top of the box with back to the goal receives a flighted ball from the right back, with the defender tight on his or her back. The player receives the ball on the chest, at the same time turning so that the ball drops just to the right; as the ball drops toward the ground, the player turns, sealing off the pressuring defender, leans, and hits a volley shot with the left foot.

a

b

c

d

Figure 2.7 *(a)* Getting chest behind the ball. *(b)* Relaxing upper body to receive ball. *(c)* Changing angle of chest to turn ball in the desired direction. *(d)* Taking a second touch out of the air as a volley to pass or shoot.

Receiving With the Thigh

Ordinarily, the thigh is used to receive balls above knee height and below chest height. As is the case when receiving with the chest, defensive pressure, if any, is usually from behind the receiving player. Pressure in front would usually prohibit allowing a ball to drop to thigh height. When receiving with the thigh, the thigh should be brought to a position parallel to the ground prior to contacting the ball (figure 2.8a). As the ball contacts the thigh, the momentum of the ball is absorbed by moving the thigh downward with the motion of the ball (figure 2.8, b-c). The angle of the thigh when the ball leaves the thigh determines the path the ball takes to the ground. Imagine trying to catch a raw egg. You prepare your hands early and try to move with the egg as you cushion it to avoid breaking the fragile shell. The soccer ball is not fragile, but the same energy-absorbing motion of the thigh takes the momentum from the ball and directs it softly toward the ground. Early preparation means raising the thigh early; the cushioning effect is accomplished by moving the thigh downward with the ball, gently slowing its momentum. The thigh should not be moving toward the ball at the moment of impact because this causes the ball to bounce upward, increasing the touches necessary to gain control of the ball.

a   b   c

Figure 2.8 *(a)* Bring the thigh up parallel to the ground before contacting the ball, then *(b-c)* absorb the momentum of the ball by moving the thigh downward with the ball's motion.

Receiving With the Instep

The instep is the most effective surface for taking a ball out of the air and preparing it to be played from the ground with the very next touch. Every other receiving surface we have described requires an additional touch to get the ball on the ground and ready to play.

When receiving with the instep, the receiver must have room to allow the ball to drop to approximately knee height or below. A low and balanced body position is again critical here to allow the receiver to adjust the free leg to the flight of the ball. The foot must be brought up to a position several feet above the ground prior to contacting the ball (figure 2.9a); the toe is pointed so that on contact the instep is parallel to the ground (figure 2.9b). The motion of the foot is similar to the motions of the thigh or the hands of someone trying to catch an egg or a water balloon. Initial contact is made with the toe pointed, and then the toe flexes as the foot moves with the flight of the ball, ideally almost catching the ball on the foot or, in most cases, simply setting the ball on the ground (figure 2.9, c-d).

a   b   c   d

Figure 2.9 *(a)* Standing in a balanced body position, the player lifts a free foot up to the ball. *(b)* Initial contact is made high. *(c)* The foot then moves with the path of the ball, *(d)* and the ball is set on the ground.

Figure 2.10 The wedged foot traps the ball between the foot and the ground.

The Wedge

The wedge technique involves using the ground as an additional surface for stopping momentum of the ball. The wedge is used primarily when a player can't get to a ball that's coming out of the air to make contact prior to the ball hitting the ground. Any time you allow a ball that's in the air to make contact with the ground, you invite the unexpected, because you can't know where the bounce might go. You often hear coaches yell, "Don't let it bounce!" When possible, it's best to follow this advice. However, on good fields, using the ground is effective if you get to a ball as it makes its way toward the ground. As the ball is about to hit the ground, the player takes the inside of the foot, toe pointed upward, and raises it above the ball so that at the moment the ball hits the ground the player makes contact on the top half of the ball. The plant leg must be bent and the center of gravity centered over that leg so that the receiver can balance and move as the ball makes contact with the ground and the other foot almost simultaneously. The receiving foot creates a wedge between the ball and the ground in which the ball is trapped (figure 2.10). The wedge technique can be effective on good surfaces, but players must master other techniques as well because the wedge is much more difficult, or even impossible, on hard, uneven surfaces or muddy fields.

Receiving With the Head

It's uncommon, but the head can also be used to receive a ball. For players to receive the ball with their head, the game situation must allow plenty of time and space because a head reception requires a second surface to get the ball to the ground. A ball served to a player wide (near the touchline) might choose to use his or her head to receive the ball to keep the serve from going out of bounds. The key, again, is in relaxing the upper body and bending the knees to absorb the momentum of the ball on contact (figure 2.11a). The contact point should be the center of the forehead, which contacts the center of the ball (figure 2.11b). The ball then drops to the feet to be settled to the ground or is volleyed out of the air.

At higher levels of play, players must learn to receive the ball in a variety of positions on the field. All of the techniques we have described can be used to receive a ball and play it in the direction the player is facing. At higher levels, a player must be able to receive a ball from behind and turn to play in an attacking direction or receive a ball from the right and prepare the ball to play to the opposite side of the field (switching the point of attack). Forwards and midfielders especially need to be able to receive the ball facing the goal they're defending and quickly face in an attacking direction to shoot, take on a defender, or make a penetrating pass in the attacking direction.

a

b

Figure 2.11 (a) Relax the upper body and bend the knees to absorb ball momentum. (b) The contact point is the center of the forehead to move the ball in the direction of the ground.

BACK-TO-GOAL AND TURNING RECEPTION

Players facing away from their goal have the unique challenge of receiving a ball in a manner that prepares them to play the ball in the direction that their team is attacking. The ultimate goal of any turning technique is to position the attacker either behind the opponent with the ball under control or facing the opponent with the ball under control as quickly and efficiently as possible (figure 2.12). The defender will be trying to keep the attacker from turning or from getting any separation from him or her. Thus, attackers must possess several techniques that allow them to adjust and respond to defenders' attempts to prevent the turn.

Figure 2.12 The goal of the turning technique is to face the defender with the ball under control.

Figure 2.13 Assume a sideways-on stance to receive the ball.

All turning techniques assume that receivers are positioned at an angle to the teammate playing them the ball in order to provide vision of the defender and space in which to turn. The attacking player should also be in a sideways-on stance to receive the ball. This stance refers to the position of the attacker's body—one foot is toward the defender and the other foot toward the oncoming ball (figure 2.13). Some players keep their back directly facing the defender, but without vision of the defender, the attacker must choose a turning option at random rather than reacting or responding to the defensive pressure. Turning techniques also use the angle and the sideways stance of the attacking player to force the defender to play on one shoulder or the other in an effort to see or steal the ball. This allows the attacking player to find space over the other shoulder in which to turn.

The tactical application of the back-to-goal or turning reception is very important because the technique is meant to take advantage of the defender's position and speed of approach. The receiver's tactical ability to read the defense is as critical as his or her ability to execute proper technique. The attacker must be comfortable taking looks over the shoulder during the execution of the techniques. Three looks are ideal: one just prior to checking for the ball, one as the ball approaches, and one immediately after the initial touch. *Checking* is the term that refers to the player moving toward the teammate with the ball, signifying a request for the ball to be played to his or her feet. In each of these looks, the attacker is trying to assess where the defender is (at what angle, how far away) and how fast (or slow) he or she is approaching. These two assessments provide the information needed to choose the proper technique to beat a pressuring defender. In the sections that follow, note the reference to the position of the defender for each technique.

Cutting the Ball Against the Grain: Defender Is Tight on the Outside Shoulder

The attacking player must first create space by trying to take the defender away from the ball. Then, as a teammate prepares to serve, the attacking player checks to the ball, creating an angle between himself or herself and the server (figure 2.14a). Looking over his or her shoulder, the attacking player can see that the defender is tight, positioned on his or her outside shoulder, and moving forward aggressively. As the ball reaches the attacking player, the player quickly makes a touch, usually with the inside of the foot farthest from the defender (figure 2.14b), and cuts with the ball in the direction opposite the defender (figure 2.14c).

a   **b**   **c**

Figure 2.14   *(a)* Attacking player creates space away from the defender and an angle between herself and the server. *(b)* The attacker makes the touch with the inside of the foot farthest from the defender, and *(c)* accelerates away from the defender.

The touch should be at an angle that puts the ball past the challenging defender, and as the player moves with the ball, his or her body should seal off the defender (figure 2.15). The touch is opposite the momentum of the defender, and the attacker must quickly accelerate away before the defender can recover.

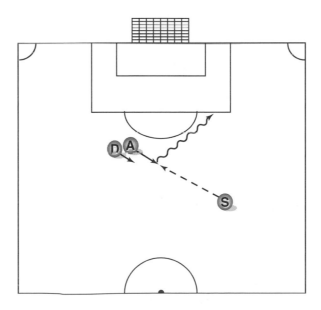

Figure 2.15   Cutting against the grain.

Dummy (Open Turn): Defender Is Tight on the Inside Shoulder

The dummy, or open turn, is set up in the same fashion as cutting the ball against the grain but is particularly effective when the defender is positioned tightly on the inside shoulder. As when cutting against the grain, the attacking player creates space, taking the defender away and checking hard to the ball as his or her teammate looks up, indicating a readiness to serve the ball. Looking over a shoulder, the attacking player again takes note of the approaching pace and distance of the defender. With the defender close and moving aggressively over the inside shoulder (usually attempting to intercept the pass), the attacking player positions himself or herself between the ball and the defender, allowing the ball to continue in the same direction but sealing off the defender's path to the ball. The receiving player must read the pace of the pass, and if the pace is slow enough, the attacking player can dummy the ball (step over the ball without touching it) and turn, sealing the defender and moving into a position with the defender behind him or her. If the pace of the pass is too much to allow the attacking player to match the pace of the ball as he or she moves off, the receiving player must open up his or her body and, with the inside of the foot farthest from the ball, take a touch that decreases the ball's pace so that he or she can move with the ball under control. The highest-level players will make this move very deceptively, changing the angle of their body as the ball approaches to keep the defender guessing which direction they intend to turn. To complete the technique, the attacking player must turn and accelerate in one motion (figure 2.16).

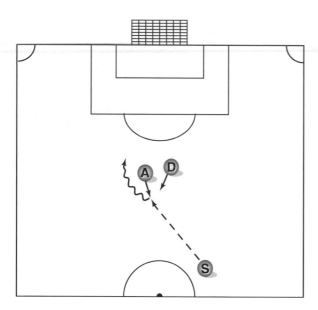

Figure 2.16   Dummy, or open turn.

Face-Up: Defender Is Staying Off a Distance

Facing-up involves turning in a tight space to face a defender who has closed the space enough to prevent the attacker from taking a forward touch but who is not tight enough to force the attacking player to play backward toward his or her own goal. In such a situation, the defender allows just enough space for a player to receive the ball and turn in one clean touch. After creating space and checking to the ball, as in all the previous techniques, the look over the shoulder allows the attacker to recognize that the defender has closed the space but is not extremely close and that the pace of approach is cautious. The attacking player can then receive the ball with the inside of the foot closest to the defender (figure 2.17a), stopping the momentum of the ball and turning to face the defender at the same time (figure 2.17b). In this case, the receiving player wants to actually stop the ball and keep it close to his or her feet to avoid penetrating toward the defender. The attacking player is now facing the defender and can immediately serve a teammate in a forward direction or accelerate toward the defender and take the player on 1v1 to attempt to get behind him or her (figure 2.17c). Often the defender will step toward the attacker to close the space, and the attacking player can use the oncoming momentum of the defender to accelerate past him or her.

Figure 2.17 *(a)* Attacking player receives with foot closest to defender, *(b)* stops and turns to face defender, and *(c)* surveys options to pass, shoot, or dribble.

Self-Pass: Defender Is at a Good Defending Distance

The self-pass technique is similar to the face-up turn, but the initial touch must be backward away from the defender to create space in which to turn and face the defender. This technique is effective when the defender is playing tight but is not raging (pressuring aggressively). Again, the receiving player is sideways on to the defender as he or she receives the ball, which provides vision of the defender and distance between the defender and the ball. First, with either the outside of the foot farthest from the defender (figure 2.18a) or the inside of the foot closest to the defender (figure 2.18b), the attacking player takes a touch away from the defender. The touch away from the defender should be five to seven yards (4.5-6.4 m) and at a pace that allows the receiving player to move with the ball and get behind it so he or she can face the defender immediately with the ball under control (figure 2.18c). Accelerating to the ball, the attacking player should reach the ball with enough time to step beyond the ball and face the defender, who is most likely moving toward the attacking player to try to prevent the separation. The acceleration to the ball after the initial touch is important to separate from the defender long enough to allow the attacking player to turn. If the touch is too short or the acceleration too slow, the defender will be able to maintain constant pressure and prevent the attacker from turning. Preventing the turn is the goal of the defensive player!

a   b   c

Figure 2.18 *(a)* Attacker takes initial touch with outside of far foot, or *(b)* attacker takes initial touch with inside of near foot. *(c)* After creating the space, the attacker steps beyond the ball and faces the defender.

RECEIVING DRILLS

Activities that provide many repetitions of passing and receiving (you can't have one without the other) always involve a small player-to-ball ratio. High repetition is necessary for improvement of any technique. Of course, executing technique in a gamelike setting is also important. As players improve their technique, the setting should become more and more realistic. There's always a tradeoff between repetition and realism, and the better the player, the greater the need for realism, including realistic pressure, realistic space, and realistic numbers. Ultimately, the game is 22 players to one ball, and receiving the ball in such an environment means assessing much more than the pace of the oncoming ball and a single defender.

Note that any activity used for passing is also great for receiving, so refer to chapter 3 for other activities to train receiving.

Split the Triangle

Purpose: To teach players to make an active first touch when receiving balls on the ground

Procedure: In partners, two to a ball, each pair sets up a triangle with cones. The object is for the players to pass back and forth in a two-touch rhythm, but each pass must go through a different side of the triangle. This activity forces players to make their first touch active in order to create an angle to play the ball through a different side of the triangle. This gets players receiving and moving with their first touch (figure 2.19).

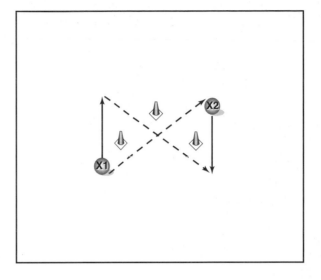

Figure 2.19 Split the Triangle.

Coaching Points: The body position of players receiving the ball should be stable, with a low center of gravity that allows them to move with the ball as they receive it. Players should use the inside and outside of both feet to receive the ball. For inside-of-the-foot receptions, the toe should be pointed up and the ankle locked. For outside-of-the-foot receptions, the toe should be angled down and inward.

Circle Up

Purpose: To practice receiving with different surfaces with little or no defensive pressure

Procedure: Divide the number of players participating into two groups. One group forms a large circle; each player forming the circle has a ball. The remaining players get inside the circle without a ball. Players on the inside check to (accelerate toward) a player on the outside who, in response, plays the ball on the ground to the checking player. The coach can instruct players to receive the ball with different surfaces, to turn or to make an active first touch and then play back to the player who initially played the ball. Here are some possibilities:

- Players receive using the inside of the foot, making a lateral touch, and then play the ball back to the player who played the first pass.
- Players receive with the outside of the foot, making a lateral touch, and then play the ball back to the player who played the first pass.
- Receivers turn and find another player on the outside who does not have a ball.

Servers on the outside can also play the ball in the air (using feet or a toss, depending on players' skill level); the options listed can then be performed with balls received out of the air.

Coaching Points: During the activity, the coach checks for proper body and foot positions for each technique. It's extremely important that players take looks over their shoulder as they check to the players in the circle. In a game situation, those looks will allow them to see the field, their teammates, and opponents so that they can make good decisions about if, when, and in what direction they can turn or make a pass.

Variation: This drill can also be done in three groups—a serving group on the circle, an attacking group working on receiving inside the circle, and a defending group (each defender paired with an attacker). The coach might instruct defenders to be passive initially and then to increase pressure until they win the ball, at which time they take the attacking role.

Horseshoes

Purpose: To practice receiving balls out of the air

Procedure: Divide players into groups of four players (two teams of two). Each group needs two flat cones and three balls. Place players from each team a set distance apart (distance depends on age and skill level). Players serve the ball in the air to their partner, who tries to take the ball out of the air and hit the other ball off the flat cone with the ball that was served. Both players from one team serve, and then both players from the other team serve (figure 2.20). Determine the number of points for victory based on the skill and ability of the players. You can play this as a 2v2 game or set the entire team up in this fashion and just play that the first team (all pairs) to reach a set number of points wins.

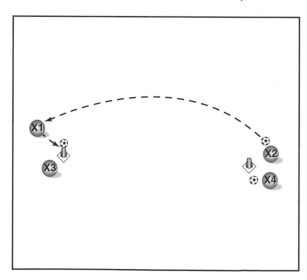

Figure 2.20 Horseshoes.

Coaching Points: This drill involves a high-level skill that can be modified for low-skilled players. The competition of the activity adds a sense of pressure. The coach should watch for players reading the flight of the ball and getting their bodies in position behind the ball; proper body and foot position; and movement of the body as players receive the ball so that the ball is directed toward the target (the ball sitting on the cone).

Variation: Players should master this game with a two-touch restriction, but the game can also be played using just one touch to take the ball out of the air and hit the ball off the cone. A one-touch game simulates making an active first touch with a ball out of the air.

Numbered Passing

Purpose: To practice receiving balls with an emphasis on preparing the ball for the next pass

Procedure: In groups of three to nine players (odd numbers work best) with one ball per group, players assign themselves a number 1 to n (total number in the group). In an open space, the players begin passing in sequence—1 to 2 to 3 to 4 to n, and then back down to 1. Once the players have the sequence established, the coach can instruct players to play in a two-touch rhythm. The goal and the coaching instruction are to make the first touch active and in the direction of the next pass. The number sequence allows the coach to evaluate whether the player prepared the ball correctly for the next pass. The coach can also instruct the group to continue in a two-touch rhythm but to play in a short-short-long sequence. Now the coach is also looking for the difference in preparation touch for a ball to be served within a short range as compared to the longer preparation touch that would be necessary to serve a longer pass.

Coaching Points: The coach should observe for proper body and foot positions. Receiving players should look before receiving so that they can find the next player in the sequence and make the first touch in that direction.

Variation: Do the drill with one group and multiple balls. The activity is the same as above except all players are in the same group. Players again are numbered 1 to n, with every fourth or fifth player starting with a ball. The better the players, the more balls can be used, up to every third player having a ball. The numerical sequence is followed as described, with the same coaching points. Now, however, pressure is increased to play cleanly and quickly. Coaches are still watching for a proper preparation touch to prepare the player for the next pass.

Technical Back to Pressure

Purpose: To practice receiving a ball with back to the goal

Procedure: In figure 2.21, players are divided into groups of four—two pairs of two, 25 to 30 yards (22.8-27.4 m) apart. Player X1 checks to player X2, who plays a pass on the ground. D1 defends X1 while X1 practices executing one of the back-to-goal receiving techniques. Initially, the defender is told where and how to defend (e.g., tight on the outside shoulder) so that the attacking player can successfully execute the desired technique. When the defender is set free, then the attacking player must make a tactical choice on how to beat or face the defender. (See chapter 8 on applying techniques tactically.)

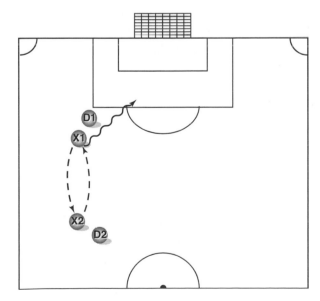

Figure 2.21   Technical Back to Pressure.

Coaching Points: The coach looks for proper body position, the check to the player in a direction that creates an angle between the server and the player receiving the ball, and players taking looks over their shoulder as they check (they should take three looks—before the check, as they accelerate toward their teammate, and after they make the first touch). The coach also watches for receivers reacting to the position, speed of approach, and distance of the defender.

MATCH-RELATED ACTIVITIES

Match-related activities put receiving (and passing) into a more realistic environment that approaches the spatial and pressure demands of an actual match. The activities without a direction (those that are for possession only) have greater repetition than those that have a sense of direction or a goal to attack. These activities have a much greater player-to-ball ratio. The shape of the players as a team influences the success of the players in this environment, so team tactics become a part of the coaching elements in these activities. These environments require using multiple receiving techniques.

5v5v5

Purpose: To practice passing and receiving with limited pressure from opponents

Procedure: Players are divided into three groups of equal size. Two groups work together to play keep away from the third group. Any time a player is responsible for the loss of possession, his or her team becomes the defending team; the team that was defending now joins the third team on the attack.

Coaching Points: Watch for players not only receiving the ball with proper technique but also protecting the ball from the defensive opponent. Players should receive the ball with an active touch away from the oncoming pressure. Players should be taking looks to sense the pressure and to locate teammates so that the receiving touch can be made in the direction of the teammate they want to pass to.

Four Square

Purpose: To practice receiving (and passing) the ball in a specific area of the field

Procedure: In a training area appropriate for the skill level and number of players, place a square about eight by eight yards (7.3 by 7.3 m) in each corner of the area (with space to play on all sides of the squares; see figure 2.22). Divide players into two even teams. A neutral attacking player(s) can be used to provide greater success and more receiving repetitions. The teams play a game of keep away, but a point is awarded each time a member of the attacking team receives a ball in the square and plays it to a teammate outside the square. A player may dribble out of the square to avoid losing the ball, but a point is not awarded. A team may not score in the same square twice in a row.

Coaching Points: This drill allows the coach to train the tactical application of the various receiving techniques. The coach should instruct players to play toward the least defended square; the receiving touch should prepare them in that direction. The receiving touch should be farther if the player has the ability to serve a longer ball; this switches the attacking space toward a different square quickly.

Variation 1: A team defends two squares and scores in the other two squares (squares can be adjacent or diagonal).

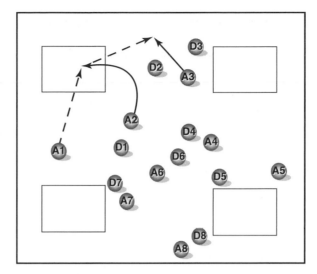

Figure 2.22 Four Square.

Variation 2: A game is the first team to score in each of the four squares. Difficulty increases as a team scores in each square, limiting their future scoring options and focusing the defensive team around fewer squares.

Three-Zone Possession

Purpose: To provide an environment that creates passing and receiving opportunities with varying amounts of space and varying amounts of defensive pressure

Procedure: As a possession game, this drill is not done with direction, giving attacking players more options but reducing the tactical decisions, because the only objective is to maintain possession. The various playing spaces create different services for the players to receive throughout the game. Begin by dividing the playing area into three zones of different sizes, numbered 1, 2, and 3. Players are split into two teams to play possession. Neutral players can be used to increase the success of possession, if necessary. Players play keep away but only in the zones that are called out by the coach. By changing the zones that are being used, the coach can control what type of balls players are receiving and serving. The coach can call "Zone 1," "Zones 1 and 2," "Zones 1, 2, and 3," "Zones 1 and 3," or other possibilities. Each combination of playing areas will promote different movement and different services (figure 2.23).

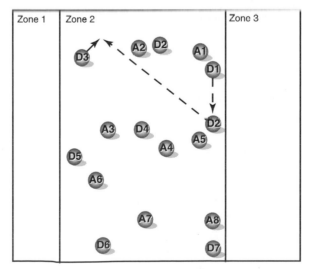

Figure 2.23 Three-Zone Possession.

Coaching Points: There's a lot for the coach to watch for in this drill. Players should position not only to receive the ball with proper technique but to protect the ball from the defensive opponent and to prepare for the pass they wish to make. They should receive the ball with an active touch away from the oncoming pressure. They should be taking looks to sense the pressure and to locate teammates so that the receiving touch can be made in the direction of the teammate they want to pass to and at the proper distance (a longer pass requires a longer preparation touch).

Back-to-Goal Receiving

Purpose: To provide attacking players with a realistic environment for training their ability to receive balls in and around the goal and to have opportunities to create goal-scoring chances

Procedure: If possible, use two large goals. Divide the playing field into two halves and play 2v2 (plus goalkeepers) in each half. Two defenders from one team and two attackers from the opposite team are in each half. As soon as they win the ball, the two defensive players or the goalkeeper look to find the attackers, who look to score as soon as possible. Any ball that goes out of bounds is restarted by the goalkeeper to keep the game moving and get even more repetitions for the attacking players. The attacking players should receive many reps of receiving balls with their back to the game and trying to turn under defensive pressure. The attackers will also be trying to receive and play the ball with a touch that allows them to shoot with the next touch.

Coaching Points: The starting position of the attacking players is important to create an angle between the attacker and the player from whom they wish to receive the ball. The coach watches for movement toward the player with the ball *or* a movement to hold the defender at bay so that the attacker clearly indicates a desire for the ball to be played into his or her feet. The attacker should take looks to determine where the defensive pressure is. Players can use deception as the ball is coming to allow attackers to get defenders off balance and possibly create an opening to take a shot. Attackers should use their body to keep defenders away from the ball. The surface choice players make for receiving the ball affects their ability to create one-touch shooting opportunities.

Variation: The two zones can be separated by a "dead zone" (an area in which no players are allowed), which forces the passes into the attacking players to be from a greater distance, which creates more opportunities to receive driven balls and balls out of the air.

GAME MODIFICATIONS TO FOCUS ON TECHNIQUE

By playing in a normal game with normal rules and regulations (even numbers, goals, and so on), players can execute technique in a matchlike environment. In this way, technique continues to progress toward becoming skill. Following are modifications or restrictions that can be placed on a normal game environment to encourage players to use the technique that is the focus of a particular training session.

- Players must make a set number of passes before they can score.
- Players can dribble only in their attacking half (encouraging players to play passes into attacking players).
- A set number of passes *or* a goal counts as a point.
- Players can shoot before four passes or after eight. This encourages a team to take advantage of a counterattack opportunity if it exists but to be patient and break down a defense if the counterattack is not available or is not successful (promotes tactical applications).

Passing

It should be simple—getting the ball from your foot to a teammate. However, sending the ball to a teammate with the right pace, the right trajectory, and the right spin is as difficult as landing a golf ball on a fast green so that it rolls just right and falls gently into the hole. Before outlining the technical elements required to execute a good pass, let's get clear on exactly what constitutes a "good" pass.

The obvious qualities of pace and accuracy are primary and vital. The ball must arrive at the feet (and at the higher levels to the proper foot) of a teammate or in a chosen space at the right speed to allow the teammate to play the ball easily or to run onto without breaking stride. However, timing and deception (making a pass at just the right moment without telegraphing it) are just as important as pace and accuracy to the success of a pass. In fact, it's timing and deception that turn the technique of passing into a functional game skill.

The demands of the game require players to use a variety of techniques to send a variety of passes. A great passer or playmaker has a large repertoire of passes. The game also demands that passes are made directly to a teammate's feet and into the desired space toward which the teammate is running. In the following sections, we use the word *target* to indicate the place (space or teammate) to which the player is attempting to play the ball.

SHORT-RANGE PASSING

The soccer field can be 80 by 120 yards (~73 by 109 m), which means that passing can take on a large variety of distances and heights. A distance considered *short range* varies depending on the age and level of the players. Generally, a pass up to about 40 yards (36.5 m) is considered short range, but for younger and less-skilled players, the distance might be shorter. Short-range passing demands accuracy and precision and is usually used to maintain possession. For example, a forward passes backward to a midfielder who is in close support, or a center back plays a ball forward through a gap to the center midfielder at an angle 20 to 30 yards (18-27 m) away. Several surfaces and several techniques can be used to connect to a teammate within that range.

Inside-of-the-Foot Pass

The inside-of-the-foot technique is most frequently used to hit a short-range pass when accuracy is vital, deception is not crucial, and pace is not a primary concern. Because this technique tends to result in the most accurate passes, it is the first technique taught to most young players. Most people are naturally inclined to kick a ball with the big toe—because the foot doesn't naturally turn outward, as is necessary to use the inside of the foot. But the toe is a small surface, so it's much more difficult to make contact with the center of the ball when using the toe. Think of a golf club—the bigger the head of the club, the bigger the sweet spot. The same principle applies to kicking a soccer ball.

Using the inside of the foot provides a large surface, which makes it easier to make good contact for a solid and accurate pass. Mastering this technique is vital for players if they are to be able to maintain possession of the ball. After mastering this technique, players then expand on their repertoire of passing to handle many situations and to add deception and variety to their passing. Used all over the field and repeatedly in a game, the inside-of-the-foot pass is the fundamental (though often overlooked) skill that provides a foundation to build on.

Whether a player is stationary or moving, the inside-of-the-foot technique is basically the same. First, the player places the plant foot to the side and fairly close to the ball; the big toe of the plant foot is pointed at the target (figure 3.1a). Second, the striking foot is rotated, and the striking leg swings from the hip away from the ball (similar to a backswing in golf; see figure 3.1b). The striking foot is held with the heel down and toe up to form a strong and large striking surface. The pace of the inside-of-the-foot pass is limited because the external rotation of the leg prevents any lower-leg snap to create foot momentum before striking the ball. Third, the striking leg swings through the ball, with the center of the inside of the foot contacting the center of the ball and the follow-through directed at the target (figure 3.1c) .

a

b

c

Figure 3.1 (a) Place the plant foot close to the ball with the big toe pointed at the target. (b) Swing the striking foot through the ball and (c) follow through to the target.

Outside-of-the-Foot Pass

This technique is similar to the inside-of-the-foot pass with respect to range and pace. However, the outside-of-the-foot pass usually has much greater spin and is more difficult to execute with accuracy. The advantage of this technique is that it is naturally deceptive (because you don't give away the direction of the pass by pointing the plant foot), which is often vital to the completion of a pass. For example, as an attacking player dribbles at a defender with a supporting teammate to the side, the dribbler can pass (with the outside of the foot) to the teammate at the last minute without the defender seeing any body signals (turning of the foot or hips). Another advantage of this technique is that as the pass is made the attacker can continue running in stride and often accelerate past the defender to receive a return pass. The outside-of-the-foot technique is quite useful in executing the traditional give-and-go (or wall pass) combination with a little deception.

To execute an outside-of-the-foot pass, a player's plant foot is pointed about 45 degrees from the intended target and farther behind the ball. The toe of the striking foot is pointed and slightly adducted (turned inward) at the moment of impact (figure 3.2a). A quick snap of the lower leg (figure 3.2b) toward the intended target, striking the center of the ball with the outside portion of the instep of the striking foot (figure 3.2c), delivers the ball to the intended target. Young or unskilled players will often attempt to produce striking power by drawing back the hip rather than by snapping from the knee to strike the ball and will get very little power. The proper technique often creates a spin on the ball, which must be taken into account when evaluating the accuracy, pace, and "friendliness" of the pass. This technique is frequently executed by a player running with the ball, adding to the functionality and deception because the defender is caught trying to intercept the pass and often allows the attacker to continue to run past him or her. Now the attacker can receive a pass back and be behind the defender.

a   b   c

Figure 3.2 *(a)* Plant foot is at a 45-degree angle to target, while toe of striking foot is turned inward at moment of impact. *(b)* Snap the striking leg quickly from the knee to produce power, and *(c)* make contact with the ball with the outside portion of the instep.

DRIVEN PASSES USING THE INSTEP

The instep pass is a technique used to deliver a ball a distance of over 30 yards (27.4 m) or to pass a shorter distance with great pace. This technique is critical when the ball needs to get to a target and get there quickly. As players increase their skills, this technique is used more frequently because speed of play becomes important. The pace of the instep pass allows a team to play faster because the ball travels faster, arrives at its target sooner, and permits a team to attack quicker. The more quickly a team can attack, the less time a defense has to recover, shift to the ball, or get behind the ball and defend.

For an instep-driven pass, the plant foot is placed directly beside the ball with the big toe pointed at the target. The striking foot is toe down and locked at the ankle (figure 3.3a). The ball is struck with the center of the instep, and the follow-through is low. The striking foot stays within a foot of the ground; the knee stays waist high or lower. The lower-leg snap (snap from the knee) is the source of the power and thus important to the pace of the pass (figure 3.3b). The swing of the leg from the hip is vital for the follow-through and accuracy of the pass but is not the source of the power. The follow-through should be straight toward the intended target (figure 3.3c). As with the outside-of-the-foot pass, young players often try to increase their power by swinging harder from the hip, which compromises accuracy while adding nothing to pace. Some players swing the leg back like a pendulum and then try to swing through from the hip with a somewhat straight leg, which decreases the power of the drive. In a proper instep drive, as the leg is taken back in preparation to strike the ball, the heel of the striking foot is brought back toward the hamstring so that the knee can snap during the kick to provide power.

a   b   c

Figure 3.3 (a) The toe of the striking foot is pointed toward the ground. (b) Snap the lower leg from the knee and (c) follow through directly toward the target.

FLIGHTED BALLS

Like the driven pass, the flighted ball is a pass over distance but uses a high trajectory, possibly to avoid defenders or to slow the ball's travel time. A midfielder trying to serve the ball over an opponent's defense to an attacker running in behind uses this technique to get the ball over the defense and allow the attacking player to run onto the ball. Once players are strong enough to strike a ball 30 to 40 yards (27-36 m), they can master this technique. Many young players can strike a flighted ball as the ball is rolling toward them, which provides momentum to get the required distance. To master the technique of a flighted pass, however, players must be able to strike (for distance) a stationary ball or a ball moving away from them.

When striking a ball into the air, the plant foot is slightly behind the ball, toe still pointed in the direction of the target. The ankle of the striking foot is locked, and the toe is turned slightly outward to allow the kicker to make contact on the lower half of the ball, which provides loft to the pass (figure 3.4a). The center of the instep strikes the center of the ball horizontally (unless a bend is desired) and the lower half of the ball vertically, with a snap of the lower leg to create power. The leg swing and follow-though are toward the target but upward to help generate the loft (figure 3.4b). The lower on the ball that contact is made, the higher the serve and the greater the backspin. Backspin is desirable if the player wants the pass to hold up once it strikes the ground.

a   b

Figure 3.4 *(a)* The ankle of the striking foot is locked and the toe turned slightly outward. *(b)* Kick with the striking foot slightly outward and make contact with the ball in the lower half to create loft, and then follow through upward toward the target.

To create backspin, the passer strikes as low on the ball as possible, almost at the point where the ball meets the ground (figure 3.5). Striking the ball in this way creates a spin on the ball toward the player striking the ball (a backspin). Backspin is often desired when a player is trying to play a ball into the space behind defenders while trying to keep the ball on the field or away from the goalkeeper. With backspin, the ball hits the ground and slows down, which allows an attacking player to run onto it without chasing it out of bounds.

CHIPS

The chip is a pass intended to get height and backspin. The distance of the chip pass is usually short because the passer only needs to get the pass over a defender. This technique can also be used as a shot on goal to play the ball over a goalkeeper who's off the goal line.

The plant foot is placed farther back and away from the ball to allow low contact with the ball. A short and choppy snap of the lower leg creates an immediate loft on the ball and excellent backspin (figure 3.6a). The toe is usually pointed and the ankle locked but slightly abducted to allow the instep to contact the ball close to the ground (figure 3.6b). There is little to no leg swing or follow-through with the chip pass.

Figure 3.5 The ball is struck as low to the ground as possible to create backspin.

a   b

Figure 3.6 (a) Use a short, choppy snap of the lower leg to create backspin. (b) At contact the toe is pointed and slightly abducted to allow the instep to contact the ball close to the ground.

BENT BALLS

Players are often required to avoid defenders or hit targets with a pass that has a curved trajectory, or a *bend*. This bend helps keep the ball away from defenders, makes it easier for teammates to receive the ball, or prevents the ball from leaving the field of play when serving near a sideline or end line (see chapter 9 on tactical application for details on using this technique effectively). Bending the ball is an advanced technique; players should master striking accurately driven and flighted passes before trying to bend balls. Once players have mastered striking flighted and driven balls, they have learned to control the contact point (the point at which the foot contacts the ball) and the follow-through, and they are then ready to work on bending the ball.

A bent ball can be driven or flighted, and the technique is almost the same as described for the driven or flighted ball without spin. The difference is the point of contact on the ball and the follow-through.

To bend a pass, contact is made slightly to the left or right of the center of the ball (figure 3.7a), and the follow-through should follow the same approximate trajectory of the desired bend of the ball (the foot makes a path with a similar shape to the path desired of the ball). To strike a ball straight, a player strikes *through* the ball. To strike a bent ball, a player strikes *across* the ball (figure 3.7, b-d). The striking foot makes contact in a similar spot as when striking a straight ball, but the trajectory of the foot follows the curved shape of the ball as opposed to striking straight through the middle of the ball. The curved motion of the striking foot creates a curved trajectory of the ball.

a   b   c   d

Figure 3.7 *(a)* Make contact slightly to right or left of the ball's center. *(b-d)* The foot strikes across the ball and should follow the same approximate trajectory of the desired bend.

PASSING DRILLS

Passing is the team skill that enables a coach to implement attacking tactics. Without passing skills, team offensive tactics are a mute point. Thus, drills that train passing skills to be progressively applied in gamelike situations are a vital part of the training regimen.

Note that any activity used to develop receiving skills can also be used to develop passing, so refer to chapter 2 for other useful activities.

2v2 Serving Drill

Purpose: To train flighted services

Procedure: Four players—a team of two in each square—face off in two squares marked off a proper serving distance apart (figure 3.8). The size of the squares and the distance between them depend on the skill level and serving ability of the players. For skilled players, the squares might be as small as 8 yards long by 8 yards (7.3 x 7.3 m) wide and 45 to 60 yards (27.4-32 m) apart, but beginning players will need larger squares with less distance between them. The drill starts with one team serving into the square of the other team. The receiving team has a set number of touches (typically three) between them to settle and serve the ball back to the opponents' square. Any combination of touches between the players is allowed. A team is awarded a point if the opposing team fails to serve the ball within the required number of touches or if the serve fails to reach the square. Play continues until one team scores a set number of points.

Coaching Points: A proper preparation touch is important to prepare the ball so players can step into the ball for placement of the plant foot and for power. Players must judge the pace of the moving ball when planting the nonstriking foot. Watch for proper placement of the plant foot, which should be slightly behind the ball at the moment of impact and pointed at the target. The contact point and the follow-through are also technical elements to evaluate. The contact point should be below the horizontal middle of the ball to get a flighted service. The follow-through should be toward the target with some upward motion to again assist in giving lift to the service.

Remember when coaching to stress the *cause* rather than the result. That is, don't say, "Strike the ball higher," or "Get the ball in the square!" Instead, focus on the technical deficiency that's causing the unwanted result. Give such instruction as, "Contact slightly lower on the ball for more height" or "Follow through toward the target to avoid the slice you just hit!"

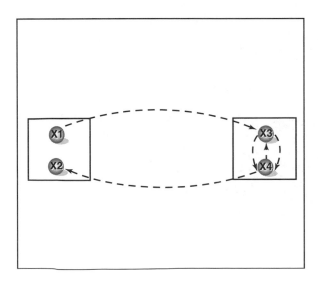

Figure 3.8 2v2 Serving Drill.

Short-Short-Long Bending Ball Rhythm

Purpose: To train serving balls at various paces and distances

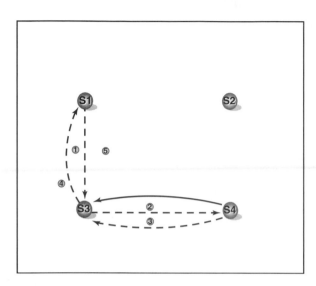

Figure 3.9 Short-Short-Long Bending Ball Rhythm.

Procedure: In groups of four, players practice serving around each other in a short-short-long rhythm. Server 1 starts by serving a ball to S3. S3 receives the pass (preferably with one touch) and plays a short pass to S4. S4 returns the pass to S3 and then pressures S3 so that he or she must play the ball around S4 in order to complete a pass to S1. S3 and S4 then switch roles. S1 and S2 combine in the same fashion so that S1 now serves around S2 to S3 and then switches roles. The combination results in a serve from S3 (that bends around S4) to S2. This sequence can be performed with driven or flighted passes that bend on the ground or in the air (figure 3.9).

Coaching Points: This activity is fundamental repetition, so the coach is looking for all technical elements described in the chapter:

- Body position
- Plant foot position
- Point of contact on the ball
- Follow-through

Variation: By instructing players not to pressure the partner who is serving the long pass, the same rhythm can be used to train serving balls without using the bending technique.

Bent Runs, Bent Balls

Purpose: To train the service of bending balls

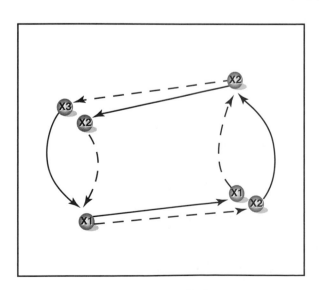

Figure 3.10 Bent Runs, Bent Balls.

Procedure: In groups of three or more (the smaller the group, the greater the fitness demands of the activity), players pass the ball in the pattern shown in figure 3.10. The coach determines the type of balls played and the direction in which the pattern is executed. The complete series includes:

- Balls on the ground bent into the path of the runner in both directions
- Balls on the ground bent with the path of the runner in both directions
- Balls flighted in the air bent into the path of the runner in both directions
- Balls flighted in the air bent with the path of the runner in both directions

The run of the player to whom the ball is served must be bent and wide, creating a passing channel for the passer.

Coaching Points: Bent Runs, Bent Balls passing is a fundamental repetition activity, but the repetition involves an advanced technique that's best suited to experienced players.

Monkey in the Middle

Purpose: To train passing with gamelike rhythm under minimal pressure

Procedure: Rhythm involves playing with a sense of purpose that makes sense for the game. For instance, short-short-long is a rhythm that brings a defensive team in tight and then attacks the space in which the defense has left itself vulnerable. Differing from the previous drill, the players (rather than the coach) will determine what types of passes to play.

Divide a playing area of about 50 yards by 25 yards (45.7 by 22.8 m) into three zones. Two of the zones (one at each end of the playing area) should be large enough for a 5v2 game of keep away, and the third zone is neutral ground in the middle. Divide players into three teams of five. Team X plays keep away from two members of team D in one of the zones at the end of the playing area. After at least three passes, team X attempts to play a long pass over or through the neutral zone to team A, which is waiting in the zone on the other end of the playing area. The other three members of team D are in the neutral zone and can intercept a pass that's traveling across the neutral zone. If the pass to the opposite zone is completed, two members of team D enter to defend in that zone, and team A plays 5v2 against team D, attempting to complete at least three passes before sending the ball back to team X in the opposite zone. If the defending team (team D in our example) wins the ball, they play the ball to the coach outside the grid, and the team that lost the ball (Team X or Team A) becomes the defending team. Two players from the new defending team come through the neutral zone to defend the team waiting in that zone, who has been played a ball by the coach (figure 3.11).

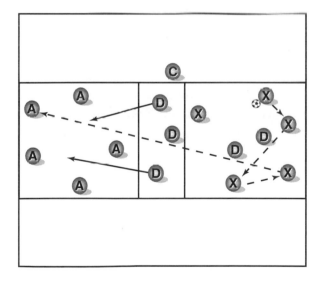

Figure 3.11 Monkey in the Middle.

Coaching Points: To keep play continuous, have a supply of balls at the side of the playing area to play into teams as necessary. Be sure to watch the plant foot, contact point, and follow-through in order to provide feedback to the players for correcting improperly served balls.

MATCH-RELATED ACTIVITIES

Match-related activities move players into gamelike environments. It's the coach's responsibility to modify environments so that the desired skill—in this case, passing—is emphasized; players need to get as many passing reps as possible. Match-related activities are critical to player development because they promote opportunities to execute a skill under realistic pressure and time constraints. These activities ensure that a *technical* player (one who has the ability to execute the technique) becomes a *skillful* player (one who can make effective use of technical abilities during games).

The match-related activities for receiving, in chapter 2, can also be used to train passing. Each environment requires repetition of both skills. The coach's challenge is to focus coaching points on the skill being emphasized. Although it's possible to work on more than one skill at a time, players benefit most from focusing on the particular skill that other activities have been targeted for during the training session. That said, a coach must understand that a good pass usually depends on a good preparation touch, which could be the receiving touch, and a player's ability to receive a ball often depends on the quality of service he or she is given. Passing and receiving are separate skills that are tightly linked during match-related activities, and even more tightly linked in actual matches. This match-related activity, called End Zone Game, focuses on making the final pass, which is typically one of the more difficult passing situations in a match.

End Zone Game

Purpose: To help players develop pace, accuracy, and timing of passes—especially the final pass into the end zone

Procedure: Players are divided into two even teams. (Neutral players can be used to create less pressure and more opportunities for possession and making the final pass.) The two teams play to an end zone on each end of the playing area. A point is scored when a team plays a pass into the end zone that a teammate is able to run onto and receive in the end zone. The player is not allowed to enter the end zone prior to the ball, forcing the passer to play a ball with the proper pace or bend to allow the teammate a chance to possess the ball in the end zone. A defender can follow a player into the end zone and win the ball for the defending team. If an attacking player strips a defender in the end zone, the attacking team continues to play but must pass the ball out of the end zone and then find a teammate running into the end zone in order to score.

Coaching Points: All of the technical elements (body position, contact point, and so on) are still correctable, coachable moments. Watch for the timing and weight of the pass into the end zone. Usually, the service into the end zone should be bent so that the ball remains in the end zone for a player to run up to or chipped so that the ball passes over the defense.

Variation: A team scoring in one end zone maintains possession to attempt to score in the opposite end zone. This is a great modification for working on transition and getting into attacking formation quickly. Players are forced to play in different areas of the field because the players who naturally float to the defensive end will be on attack as soon as the direction changes. This modification is difficult for younger players because the direction of attack changes frequently, which can cause confusion.

Shooting

The coach never has to encourage players to practice shooting. Of all the techniques in the game, shooting is by far the favorite and most practiced. The coach's challenge is to make shooting practice realistic to what players will experience in a real game. Once the basic technique of striking a soccer ball correctly is accomplished, the coach must involve players in the types of shooting practices that will transfer to what they experience in game conditions.

All players can improve their ability to shoot and finish. Once the basic elements of ball striking are mastered, shooting and finishing effectively is a matter of practice. As always, whenver possible practice should mimic what players will experience in games. However, sometimes players might find themselves alone with only a bag of balls, and practice can still take place. In such a case, they should practice hitting shots on moving balls. A drill for a player to run through individually might go something like this: Have a pile of balls 20 yards (18.2 m) from goal in the center of the field. Roll one to the right, run to it, and strike it at the goal. Jog back and toss the next one into the air, then try to volley or half-volley the ball toward the goal. Ways to practice alone are limited only by the player's imagination.

If a player can find even one friend to come out and practice shooting and finishing, they will enjoy practice more and stick with it longer. Now one player can pass to another while they practice finishing crosses, playing balls on the ground or in the air, playing through passes, angled passes, and even headers. They might finish a session with a series of 1v1 duels to goal.

SHOOTING WITH POWER AND ACCURACY

Figure 4.1 Close hip and strike through the ball parallel to the ground.

The basic technique of striking a soccer ball cleanly with the instep is the foundation for shooting with power and accuracy. Striking the ball cleanly includes loading and unloading the kinetic chain through a rotary component of closing the opened hip, followed by a linear action that allows the instep to strike through the ball with a trajectory that is parallel (or a degree or two above parallel) to the ground (figure 4.1). A key factor in the player's visualization process is to imagine the instep striking through the center of the ball on a line to the intended target.

General guidelines for striking the ball more powerfully include the following:

- Tightening the muscles that act on the ankle joint
- Taking a longer hop onto the supporting foot
- Making a concerted effort to more explosively extend the knee joint

You might have noticed that when you want to make a shorter instep pass, the muscles that act on the ankle joint will soften, just as your hands soften in golf when hitting a short pitch to the green. But when striking a long ball or hitting a powerful shot, the muscles that act on the ankle joint will tighten, just as the mucles of the hand tighten when gripping a hammer to pound a large nail into a thick board.

When taking a powerful shot, also make a conscious effort to more explosively snap the knee to make that lever of the lower leg and rigid, stiff ankle crush the instep through the ball.

Shooting the ball is usually initiated with a run-up of three or four steps, approaching the ball from an angle of 5 to 10 degrees to the target line (figure 4.2) Coming from this slight angle allows a smooth strike of the ball full on the instep.

Another critical element in striking the ball is the hop onto the support (nonkicking) foot. The hop allows time for the kinetic chain to load the hip and cock the kicking leg prior to striking the ball. The support foot lands 10 to 12 inches (about 25 to 30 cm) laterally from the ball (figure 4.3). Although many coaches teach that the support foot should land beside the ball, a more precise placement is a line through the junction of the foot and big toe of the support foot, running across and through the center of the ball. Also, make sure that the knee of the support leg is flexed at contact (figure 4.4). A flexed knee facilitates the ability to drive the striking foot through the ball and achieve a strike that stays parallel to the ground. This parallel strike is vital to keeping the shot low.

Figure 4.2 Run up three or four steps at a 5- to 10-degree angle.

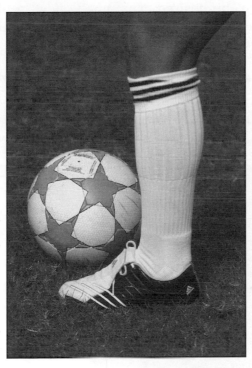

Figure 4.3 Hop and land about 12 inches laterally from the ball.

Figure 4.4 Flex support knee at contact.

Following Through the Shot

In an efficient follow-through, the kicking foot follows the target line, and the momentum from a powerful strike pulls the support foot off the ground, also along the target line. If the ball is struck cleanly, the player lands on the kicking foot, with body propelled along the target line. Visualize a round, compact body driving the kicking foot through the center of the ball and continuing along the target line.

Both player and coach can monitor the correctness of the strike by observing the spin on the ball as it flies through the air. A ball struck cleanly will have either no spin or a slight bit of backspin A ball struck in this manner flies straighter through the air and travels at a faster velocity. A ball spinning laterally (sidespin) has not been struck correctly and bends in the direction of the spin. When a player strikes the ball, the foot must travel through the midline of the ball along the target line. If the knee points outward at contact, the foot will hit through the ball on a line to the outside of the intended target line. Typically, this occurs when players approach the ball at too great an angle in an effort to strike the ball on the instep, and the resulting contact occurs with the kneecap and the instep pointing to the outside of the target line. While a soccer player often wants to make the ball bend, learning the proper technique of powerfully driving the ball at goal is the first objective.

The most common error in not striking the ball cleanly is termed *falling off the ball*, which occurs when a player finishes with a sideways, falling motion to the left as the right foot crosses over the left on the follow-through (figure 4.5). The body should become like a cannonball, driving the instep through the center of the ball and continuing along the target line.

To achieve the desired cannonball effect, a player should approach the ball straighter on than normal (closer to the intended target line) and focus on keeping the kneecap pointed at the target. This helps ensure that the instep will drive through the ball along the target line and the whole body will finish the strike moving toward the target. The upper body will have a slight curl. With the shoulder of the kicking foot moving over the point at which the ball was struck, the cannonball effect will result (figure 4.6).

Figure 4.5 Player falls left and right foot crosses over left leg.

Figure 4.6 Upper body has sligh curl and the kicking foot shoulder moves over the point of contact.

Keeping the Head Steady

The shooter needs to make a focused effort to keep the head steady while shooting. A steady head permits the player to focus on a spot on the ball. Like the golfer who picks a dimple on the back of the ball that he or she wants the club to strike through, the shooter focuses on a spot on the back of the ball that he or she wants to strike with the instep. Again, focus on continuing the strike through the center of the ball. When putting, the golfer will mark a straight line on his or her ball that is adjusted to a point down in the intended line of the putt. The shooter must imagine a line on the ball, with his or her foot striking the back of the ball and continuing through the ball on the target line. A steady head allows the eyes to focus sharply on the ball and imagine this line as the ball is struck.

After players can strike a clean, stationary ball, they're ready to practice shooting moving balls while on the move. They should work on shooting balls coming from all angles, along the ground, and in the air. All of these techniques must be learned if all shots on goal are to be strongly finished.

FINISHING

Let's make sure we're clear on terminology. To this point we have been discussing the process of shooting, which usually connotes a hard, powerful strike of the ball with the instep, struck from a distance. A more definitive term we'll now use is *finishing*, which is the way a player strikes the ball at the goal. The finish might be an explosive shot from 25 yards out or completing a chance by bending a ground ball around and past the goalkeeper. The powerful instep kick is the basis for most finishing.

Shooting for Power

When first learning to shoot, it's usually best for players to shoot for power. Aim at the goalkeeper's knees and strike the ball as hard as you can. During Andre Agassi's development, he was encouraged to hit a tennis ball very hard. With practice and maturity, he was eventually able to hit powerful, penetrating ground strokes with great accuracy. Likewise, soccer players should learn to strike the ball very hard when shooting. If accuracy is crucial, they should take a *little* velocity off the ball but still make a hard shot.

While developing, players should spend a lot of time practicing powerful strikes on goal. Such training strengthens the precise muscle groups used when shooting. Over time, as these muscle groups become more powerful, players will be able to shoot explosively from greater distances, from off-balance body positions, and from acute angles. Eventually, players will become a threat to score from all over the field.

When describing the powerful instep drive as the basis for shooting, the coach might compare striking a soccer ball with hitting a golf ball or tennis ball. The flight of a soccer ball, golf ball, or tennis ball is determined by the angle of the implement (foot, club or racket) as it strikes the ball, the line along which the implement strikes, and at which point (above or below the ball's centerline) the ball is struck. Players should visualize the kicking foot as a striking implement; by using different surfaces of the foot, hitting along a specific line, and hitting a specific spot on the ball, they can select the ball's flight characteristics.

The coach begins with a stationary ball, progresses to a moving ball, and then introduces defenders. Once players can finish well in a simple environment, the coach adds complexity by introducing defenders and making the exercises more gamelike. The closer the coach can simulate a real-game environment, the better the training is, and the better it will transfer to games.

After mastering the basic instep kick, players need to practice using the inside of the instep and the outside of the instep as striking surfaces. Both surfaces are used for control and to make the ball bend during its flight.

Finishing Complex Shots

Once they have mastered a variety of shooting techniques, players should work more on finishing a moving ball while on the move. Progress training from simple to complex. Players begin by finishing rolling balls, then move to finishing balls in the air and, finally, to mastering side-volleys.

Shots on the Ground   Shooting balls that are rolling along the ground requires the player to make a concerted effort to plant the support foot so that at contact the support foot will be close (approximately one foot) to the ball. The strike is a shorter stroke than with a standing ball, as the momentum of the rolling ball will help to add pace to the shot. The shooter must determine the best surface of the foot to strike the ball based on the angle he or she approaches the ball and the angle at which the ball is arriving.

Figure 4.7 Strike the ball from behind with the instep before it touches the ground.

Shots in the Air   Players are often required to finish shots that are in the air. Shooting a ball in the air is called a *volley*. The volleying surface is the instep. The volley is a difficult skill, so training best begins with a simple exercise in which the shooter comes from straight behind the ball, allows the ball to drop, and strikes it just before it would hit the ground. The lower the shooter allows the ball to drop, the more power and looping action will result (figure 4.7). Once players can execute the front volley, they should progress to executing the front volley from different distances and angles.

Side-Volley Shots The side-volley might be the most technically difficult shot to perform. In figure 4.8, the technique shows the shooter with the thigh raised and parallel to the ground. As the leg is raised to the parallel position, the volley is executed with knee extension and the instep hitting through the ball.

Figure 4.9, a-c, shows the sequence of events in a side-volley. The preparatory move loads the body like a backswing to strike the ball (figure 4.9a). The arms, shoulders, and hips turn backward to load the kinetic chain. In figure 4.9b, the left foot plants, and the right leg is lifted parallel to the ground with the kneecap pointing at the target. The unloading of the chain can be visualized as something like a discus thrower just before releasing the discus. The difference is that the body leans down to the left as the right leg whips around the axis of the body. In figure 4.9c, the loading and unloading have prepared the right foot (through knee extension) to strike through the ball above the ball's centerline. This helps keep the shot low.

Once players have mastered the basic technique of the side-volley, the coach can vary the length, angle, and height of the toss to add difficulty. With the basic shooting technique in place, gamelike shooting exercises that simulate what players will experience in games should be introduced.

Figure 4.8 Raise thigh to parallel, extending knee, and strike with instep.

The ability to shoot and finish is the most important skill in soccer. Soccer is a low-scoring game because of the difficulty of scoring. The sophistication of modern defensive systems and the evolution of today's goalkeeper have made scoring even more difficult. A player with the natural ability to score goals is rare and commands the highest salaries in today's ultracompetitive professional soccer world.

a   b   c

Figure 4.9 (a) Load the body by turning the arms, shoulders, and hips backward. (b) Plant your foot and lift the kicking leg parallel to the ground, then (c) strike through the ball's centerline.

SHOOTING DRILLS

It is the intrinsic motivation of players to practice skills—in this case shooting—on their own that leads to good performance in training sessions. A more skillful player expands the tactical teaching possibilities for the coach.

With a little creativity, players can imitate many of the types of scoring chances that occur during games. They might begin with stationary balls placed in strategic scoring positions in and around the box. Try placing many balls in one location to practice a certain shot from a certain angle or distance. Experiment with different surfaces—instep, inside and outside of the instep, toe pokes, bends one way or the other, and so on.

The coach should include shooting training for all players as often as possible. Forwards particularly must do some form of shooting or finishing training every session. Further, ensure that as many exercises as possible culminate with a shot at goal and that goalkeepers take part in all shooting training.

Because the focus is shooting, clean striking of the ball will be practiced by shooting at the goal, as opposed to a back or midfield player who may be practicing a long pass upfield to a forward.

Implicit in the need to provide as many repetitions as possible is the necessity for each repetition to be done correctly. The coach may use the same exercise to elicit different outcomes. Using this same exercise to emphasize fitness would require the player to shoot the 10 balls as quickly as possible by sprinting immediately to the next ball after each one is shot. Because this is fitness training, we are interested in how fast the player can shoot the 10 balls. Fitness training emphasizes how many shots per unit of time are struck, and quality is a secondary goal.

Performing this exercise for technical training emphasizes, again, the quality of each repetition. Fewer participants allow the coach to spend more time observing and correcting each player's technical execution.

Stationary Shooting

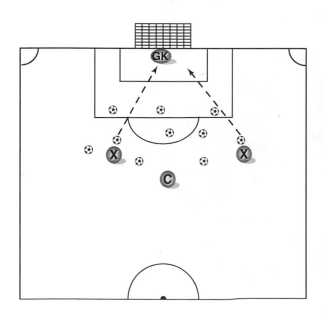

Figure 4.10 Stationary Shooting.

Purpose: To improve shooting technique using a stationary ball

Procedure: Place 10 balls randomly at distances and angles appropriate for the age and experience level of the shooter (figure 4.10). The shooter moves from ball to ball, shooting at goal. Because the focus is on technical training (rather than endurance training), the shooter takes time to move to the next ball and stops before each shot. Stress the quality of each repetition. Shooters focus on the quality of striking each ball. To ensure that technique is correct, the first exercise is with a stationary ball, and the coach addresses only the correct technique of shooting. Any number of players can participate in this drill, but of course the fewer the players, the more repetitions each shooter will get.

Coaching Points: Focus feedback on technical training. Corrections should be simple and singular—too much information will clutter and impede the players' thought and striking processes.

Finishing Ground Balls

Purpose: To practice using the appropriate foot and appropriate surface of the foot for shots on the goal

Procedure: Place six balls around the periphery of the box. Balls will be rolled toward the penalty spot for players to finish. Players line up behind three cones, as shown in figure 4.11. As balls are played toward the space between the penalty spot and the top of the box, players shoot at goal using the appropriate foot and appropriate surface. Players change starting positions after each attempt at goal.

Coaching Points: Players should always shoot with the foot closer to the ball. Players should not let the ball run across the body to the opposite foot.

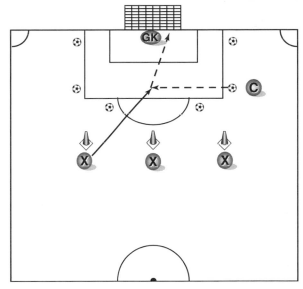

Figure 4.11 Finishing Ground Balls.

Bending the Shot

Purpose: To practice bending the ball using either the inside or the outside of the instep

Procedure: Cones are placed at an angle that requires the shooter to use either the inside or outside of the instep (figure 4.12). Player 1 starts outside the first cone and dribbles inside (goal side) the cone closest to the goal. This angle sets up the shooter to bend the ball from right to left, by striking the outer half of the ball with the inside surface of the instep. Player 2 will likewise start outside the first cone and dribble inside the cone closest to the goal. This angle sets up that player to bend the ball from left to right by striking the outer half of the ball with the outside of the instep.

Coaching Points: Any number of players can participate in the exercise and should alternate sides.

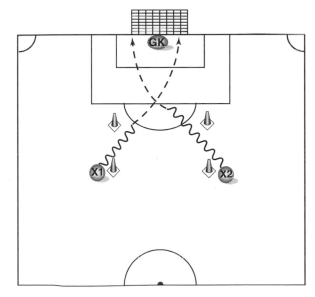

Figure 4.12 Bending the Shot.

Volley on the Bounce

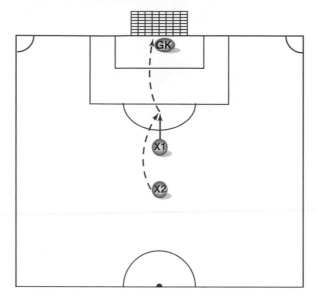

Figure 4.13 Volley on the Bounce.

Purpose: To improve volleying technique

Procedure: The front volley is practiced by tossing the ball from behind and over the head of player 1 (figure 4.13). Player 2 tosses the ball with two hands in an underhand fashion. The ball arcs over player 1, who allows the ball to bounce once and then volleys it from behind.

Side-Volley

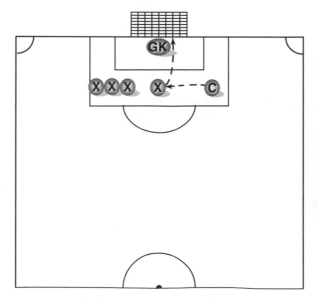

Figure 4.14 Side-Volley.

Purpose: To practice getting thigh parallel with ground and kneecap pointing at target in preparation for side-volley

Procedure: The coach asks the first player in line to stand just behind the penalty spot. He or she tosses the ball in a small arc from 10 feet away (figure 4.14). In the initial phase, the ball should arc no higher than the shooter's head. The technique demands that the shooter lift his or her leg and strike the ball with the instep.

4v4 in Box With Support Players

Purpose: Using repetition to practice shots in a gamelike scenario

Procedure: Four attackers play against four defenders. Four additional players are placed outside the box to act as support players. The coach has a supply of balls, and the attackers will always get the next ball from the coach. The coach varies the service to the attackers. They must find a way to shoot. They can dribble, pass to each other, or pass to one of the support players. The support players can deliver any type of pass or cross for the attackers to shoot. With three groups of four, the coach rotates the groups every two to four minutes (figure 4.15).

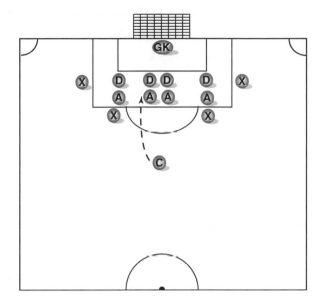

Figure 4.15 4v4 in Box With Support Players.

4v4 With Support Players

Purpose: To develop shooting skills under pressure of defenders and transition to defending

Procedure: Two goals are placed a little farther apart than the depth of two penalty boxes (figure 4.16). Again, the exercise has four attackers and four defenders inside the playing area. Around the periphery are four more attackers and four more defenders. The line of attackers shoots at one goal, and the line of defenders shoots at the other. Whichever team is not in possession of the ball becomes the defending team. The line of attackers may use the four attackers on the outside of the space, and the line of defenders may use the additional four defenders.

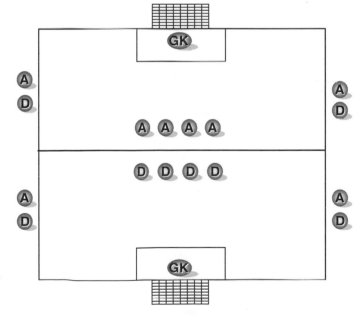

Figure 4.16 4v4 With Support Players.

After four or five minutes, the eight players in the shooting space change places with those outside. The coach has a supply of balls and always starts the next repetition.

Distance Shooting

Purpose: To develop shooting skills at long distances

Procedure: A space is laid so that its length is a little more than the depth of two penalty boxes (36-40 yards); figure 4.17a. Goals are set up at either end of this playing area and a halfway line is marked. On one side of the halfway line, a defender plays against three attackers. In the other half, an attacker plays against three defenders. No one may cross the halfway line. The goalkeeper of the attacking team starts by rolling a ball to one of the three attackers on his or her side. The object is for the attackers to shoot at the defenders' goal and vice versa. Again, no one may cross the halfway line. The attackers may pass to each other to shoot or pass to their teammate on the other half of the field to make a shot attempt. The teammate on the other half can also pass the ball back to teammates to take the shot. On each half of the field there will always be a 1v3 setup.

Variation 1: The numbers are increased by adding another attacker and defender to make competition 2v3 in each half. The options can be increased by allowing one of the three to cross the halfway line if he or she first forwards the ball to a teammate in the other half. Figure 4.17b shows attacker 3 receiving a ball from attacker 2, dribbling forward, and then playing a pass across the halfway line to attacker 4, who wall passes the ball back to attacker 3. Attacker 3 can cross the halfway line to shoot because he or she played the ball off a teammate in the attacking half.

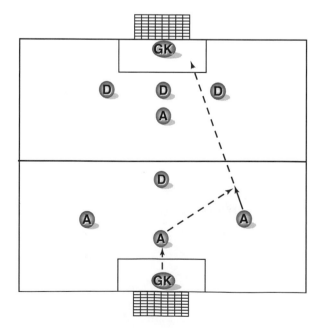

Figure 4.17a Distance Shooting.

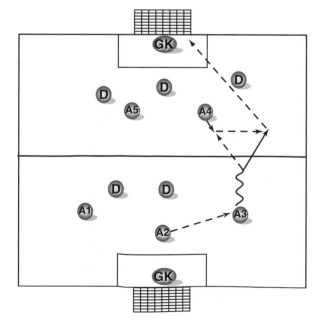

Figure 4.17b Distance Shooting, variation 1.

Variation 2: Four servers are added to stand in each corner (figure 4.17c). The task of the server is to cross the ball into the box for the attacking team to score. The options now are these:

1. Attacker 1, 2, or 3 may shoot the ball.

2. The ball may be forwarded by attacker 1, 2, or 3 to one of their teammates on the opposite side, who may then dribble and shoot, combine with each other to shoot, or lay the ball back to attacker 1, 2, or 3 to shoot.

3. Attacker 1, 2, or 3 may go into the other half to make it 3v3, if he or she forwards to attacker 4 or 5 first.

4. Any attacker in either half may play a ball wide for one of the servers to cross.

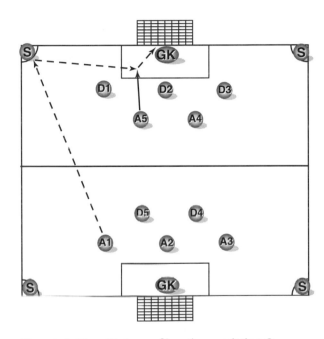

Figure 4.17c Distance Shooting, variation 2.

5

Heading

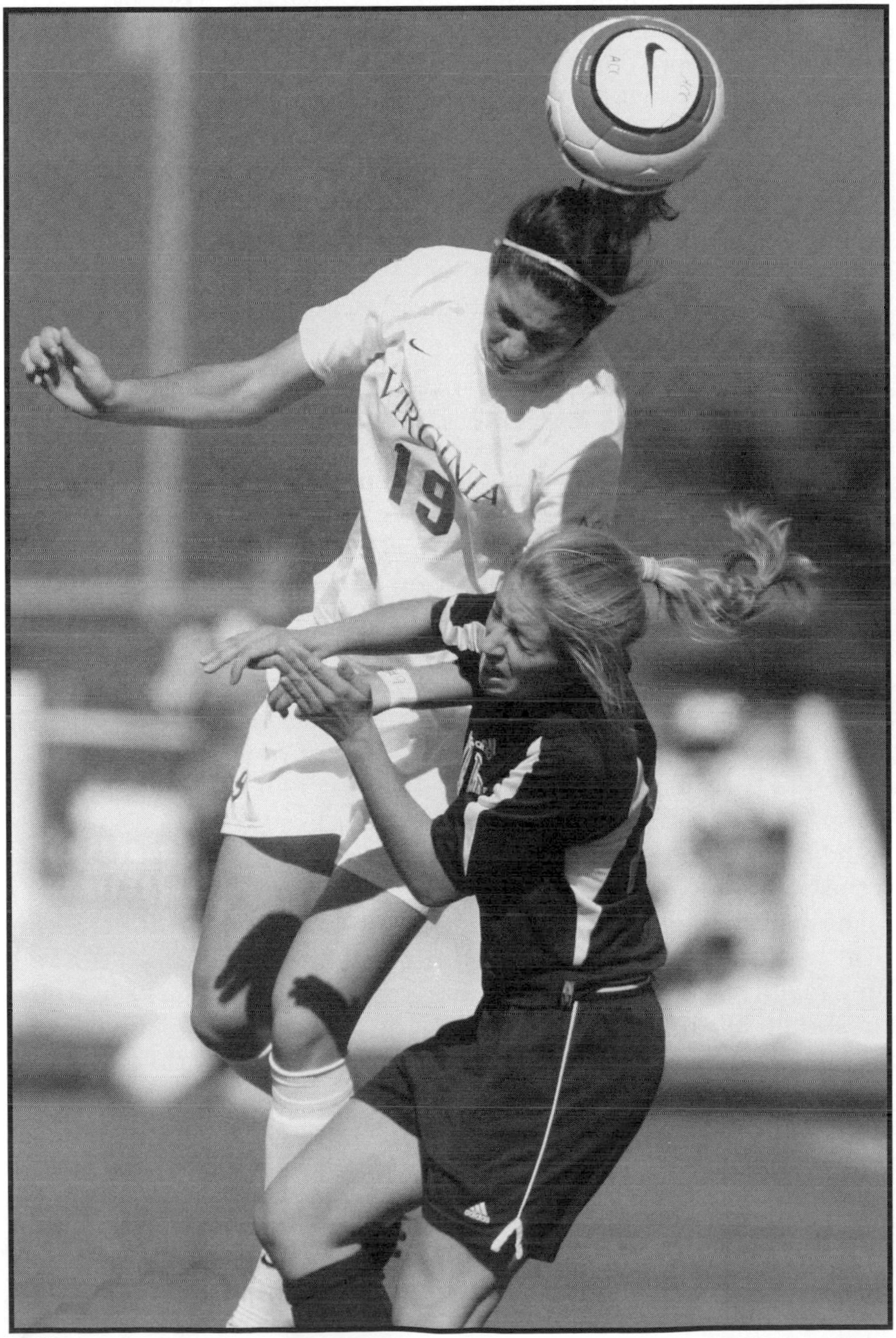

One of the most unique skills in all of sport is heading a soccer ball. People who don't play soccer marvel at the skill and ask the typical questions: "Doesn't it hurt?" and "How do soccer players do that?"

How frequently soccer players choose to head the ball can be influenced by weather conditions and surface and size of the field. If enough rain has fallen to create mud or puddles, players can't pass the ball effectively on the ground, so they resort to playing the ball through the air, which obviously results in more heading opportunities. If the surface of the field is rough and bumpy, tactics again demand bypassing the ground and playing balls in the air. Likewise, a small field means defenders are closer together, which means it's more difficult to play the ball on the ground, so the tactical answer is to play defenders out of the game through the air. These conditions multiply the opportunities and necessity of heading and thus create a much more combative style of game because players are constantly in 1v1 duels to jump against one another and battle for the ball.

With an eye on safety, heading should be included frequently in training. Heading is an integral part of the game, and players must know how to head safely and competently as the tactical situation demands. Those with special heading talents (usually the taller players) should be encouraged to practice their specialty, whether it is defensive heading in the center of a zonal back four or getting on the end of crosses, corners, and free kicks to head to goal.

DEVELOPING HEADING SKILLS

Heading is a special skill that when performed correctly is a valuable tool in a soccer player's technical arsenal. Soccer players might have to head the ball many times in a game. Some games can feature up to 75 opportunities to head the ball. Heading opportunities occur most frequently in the final thirds of the field.

Powerful heading can be likened to the shooting of a bow and arrow. As the arrow is drawn back by an archer, the string pulls both ends of the bow into a curve and loads the bow. When the arrow is released, the energy of the bow straightening propels the arrow forward. You can see the same mechanics operating when soccer players jump to head the ball. As they jump, prior to striking the ball, the head and shoulders bend backward slightly and are counterbalanced by the legs flexing at the knees (figure 5.1a). This loads the body like the flexed bow. To strike the ball, the head and shoulders are propelled forward, and the legs will also move forward as the body unloads to strike the header (figure 5.1, b-c).

The initial stage in developing proper heading technique requires familiarity with the striking surface. To head the ball, the player must strike the ball in the same manner as when shooting or passing. The striking surface must be held firm and should hit through the ball along the target line. The head is held firmly by the conscious contraction of the neck muscles, which rigidly positions the forehead to strike through the ball. Striking above or below the equator or along the side of the ball allows the header to purposely alter its flight path.

The striking surface is the middle of the forehead at the hairline. At impact, the muscles of the neck and shoulders contract and propel the striking surface through the ball.

Because heading is a complex motor skill, the coach should use a "building block" technique in the teaching process. The building block technique begins with iso-

Figure 5.1 *(a)* Bend head and shoulders back while flexing knees, and *(b)* propel head and shoulders forward as legs move forward. *(c)* The striking surface is the middle of the forehead.

lating the movement of the head and neck. Next, the flexion and extension of the trunk are added to the motion of the head and neck. The third step has the player heading a ball held overhead by a partner that allows the header to connect the three blocks into a complete heading motion.

Building Block 1: Isolating Head and Neck Movement

For the first building block, the player sits on the ground with knees flexed and relaxed. The coach or one of the player's teammates throws a soft, underhand toss for the seated player to head back into the tosser's hands (figure 5.2a). The focus of this initial building block is to ensure that the header is using the correct striking surface—the forehead at the hairline. The header must understand that he or she is striking the ball with the head. The ball does not hit the head; rather, the head strikes the ball. As the ball is tossed, the header pulls back the head like a rattlesnake preparing to strike its victim. The strike of the header is an explosive projection of the head and neck that propels the forehead through the ball along the target line (figure 5.2b). The hips and trunk are relatively stationary during this first building block.

The hands and arms come from a resting position in the lap prior to the toss to a position in which they are parallel with the shoulders, elbows flexed, and act as a counterbalance when striking the ball. The parallel shoulder position also mimics the correct position of the arms to ward off opponents when dueling for the ball in the air.

a   b

Figure 5.2 *(a)* Coach tosses ball to player sitting on ground, and *(b)* the player strikes ball explosively with head and neck.

The header attempts to head the ball back into the tosser's hands at waist to chest height. By striking the ball slightly below its equator (centerline), the ball will be headed upward. By striking the ball above its equator, the ball will be headed downward. The coach should reinforce that the eyes are to remain open throughout contact (the eyes will, however, blink reflexively on contact) and that the mouth stays closed to prevent biting the tongue. The coach should also reinforce that the toss is thrown in a soft arc that allows the header time to withdraw the head and neck and then attack the ball.

Because this is technical training, the coach is interested in the quality of each repetition. There should be no urgency to rush through the tosses. The tosser takes time to allow the header to relax momentarily before the next toss. The header should head only six to eight balls before exchanging roles with the tosser. Heading only six to eight balls allows the header to fully concentrate on the *quality* of each header.

There are two advantages to the first building block. The first is that the short toss allows the header to overcome any fear of heading the ball. Some young players are fearful of heading a soccer ball, but the short, soft toss usually allays those fears because the ball–head contact is not severe enough to cause any discomfort.

A second advantage of the first building block is that the coach can positively reinforce players when they head the ball. Success is relatively easy in this first stage, and players love nothing more than to be praised by the coach.

Building Block 2: Flexing and Extending the Trunk

The second building block begins with the header in a kneeling position (figure 5.3a), which allows the header to add trunk flexion to the projection of the head and neck. As the ball is tossed, the header bends the trunk back to load the trunk and head. The arms rise to the parallel-shoulder, elbows-flexed position described in the first building block. The heading motion is a whipping forward of the trunk and projection of the neck as the head strikes through the ball (figure 5.3b). The momentum of heading through the ball will cause the player to fall forward onto his hands (figure 5.3c); this second building block really gives a player the feeling of heading a soccer ball. The ball can now be struck hard, and the coach can focus on the trajectory of the header. The coach might ask the player to head a series of balls up, then a series down, or alternate one high and then one low. Again, the tosser and header should switch roles every six to eight headers. The objective remains the quality of each head ball.

a   b

c

Figure 5.3   (a) Header starts in kneeling position. (b) After loading the trunk and head, the trunk whips forward and neck projects as head strikes through the ball, and (c) the player falls onto his hands.

After success is achieved in the second building block, the tosser may be asked to toss the ball and then take a couple of quick steps to the side. The header will then attempt to head the ball to the tosser in his or her new position. The tosser must toss the ball from straight on and take only one or two steps to the side. The header now must head the ball to the right or left of center. It's important that the header still strikes the ball with the same heading surface—the middle of the forehead at the hairline. The coach should reinforce the correct striking surface and not permit players to use the side of their head. To head successfully to the tosser requires only that the header slightly rotate his or her shoulders and trunk.

The coach can now ask players to head up, down, or to the right or left. The tosser can ask for a series of headers that are all headed to the same place or alternate headers to different targets. The header now also has the options of heading high left, low right, and so on.

The final stage in the second building block introduces some decision making by the header. The tosser stands a little farther back to add time of flight to the toss. After throwing, the tosser moves to the right or left or stands still. The tosser also holds his or her hands high or low. The header must decide where to head and then technically execute the correct header to hit the target. The target is always the tosser's hands.

Building Block 3: Heading a Stationary Ball

For the third building block, the tosser stands with the ball held overhead. The coach should monitor the size of the holder and header. The holder must be at least as tall or taller than the header. The holder holds the ball high overhead with arms extending the ball slightly forward as well as overhead (figure 5.4a). The header will stand underneath and just behind the ball.

The header now jumps and heads the ball being held in the holder's hands. The header should jump straight up from a two-foot takeoff in preparation to strike the ball. There is a rhythm to the jumping and heading that can be described as *jump, hang, strike!* The jump is the explosive jumping motion of the legs that propels the body upward. The arms assist by lifting explosively. The arms will also open, elbows flexed, into the position described in building blocks 1 and 2.

The hang occurs as the header is reaching the apex of the jump. The hang is analogous to a baseball player, tennis player, or golfer who experiences that split-second pause between the backswing and the transition to the forward swing, or downswing. As the apex is reached, the header has loaded the body by the backward bending of the truck and the rattlesnake-like coiling of the head and neck. The legs flex slightly at the knees, and the header resembles the letter *C* at the apex of the jump and hang (figure 5.4b).

The jump and hang have prepared the header's body to apply an explosive strike to the ball with the unloading of the trunk and head, as in building blocks 1 and 2 (figure 5.4c).

Seen in slow motion, there's a definite rhythm to the jump, hang, and strike when jumping to head the ball. The header's target is just below the equator of the ball. He or she attempts to powerfully strike the ball, trying even to head the ball through the hands of the holder. The header must jump straight up and not jump forward into the holder. The emphasis is for the header to achieve the rhythm of jump, hang (loading), and strike (the actual explosive unloading to hit through the head).

a

b

c

Figure 5.4 (a) Header stands underneath the hands of the tosser and the extended ball. (b) The header loads the body at the apex of the jump and (c) strikes the ball explosively.

Figure 5.5 One-foot takeoff prior to heading.

Once again, the coach should reinforce that this is technical training and that the header should take enough time between each repetition of jump, hang, and strike. After a repetition is completed, the header should relax, compose him- or herself, and then begin to concentrate for the next repetition.

An advanced stage in the third building block is for the header to stand a couple of steps away from the holder and take a short run up to facilitate a one-foot takeoff prior to heading the ball (figure 5.5). A one-foot takeoff enables the header to jump higher, which is certainly advantageous in dueling with opponents in the air.

The most difficult part of this advanced stage will be the header's ability to translate the horizontal component of the run-up to the vertical component of jumping. The header must really concentrate on this transition to jumping vertically because it will facilitate outjumping opponents and prevent the fouling that occurs when headers jump into opponents.

WINNING HEAD BALLS

The progression for successfully winning head balls begins with players dealing with the line of flight of the ball. They want to get into the line of flight so that they can attack the ball along a 180-degree line. The player's concentration is not on the opponent but on the path of the ball and getting into the line of flight to attack the ball. A player can always jump higher with a one-foot takeoff preceded by a short run-up, so every effort is made to find a path to the ball that allows a couple of steps followed by a one-foot takeoff. This may require even stepping away from the opponent, but if the line of flight is determined early, the header can attack the ball with an explosive one-foot takeoff. As the header jumps to head, his or her arms should explosively lift to shoulder height to help gain elevation. At the same time, the arms should extend out to the side of the body, elbows flexed, parallel with the shoulders to create a cone of space around the header that simultaneously wards off the opponent and allows the header an unobstructed path to strike the ball (figure 5.6).

To gain space in the air, the header is making a concerted effort to translate the horizontal stepping

Figure 5.6 Player creates cone of space.

component into a vertical jumping component. Jumping first and making the body as big as possible prevents the opponent from entering the space in which the ball is coming down. Striking the ball at the apex of the jump further ensures winning the head ball.

Although it is always preferable to execute a short run-up or a couple of steps for a one-foot takeoff, there are times when a player can't achieve any sort of run-up. When players must head a ball while standing still, they should use a two-foot takeoff. The rest of the technique is the same—deal with the line of flight of the ball (not the opponent); jump explosively, using the arms to help gain lift; and create a cone of space with wide arms parallel to the shoulders. Make every effort to jump before the opponent and strike the ball at the apex of the jump.

It is during the jump that the bow and arrow action is used to powerfully strike the ball. As the player is jumping, he or she is arching the body as if drawing a bow. At the apex of the jump, the head, shoulders, and trunk explode forward to strike the ball. The legs flex backward on loading and extend forward to counterbalance the body as the head strikes the ball.

Heading on Defense

Defending players will be called on to head long balls played out of the opponents' defense to their forwards; they will have to head crosses from the flanks as well as head corner kicks and free kicks. A frequent header is required when the opponent goalkeeper punts the ball or has to take a goal kick. For defenders, the long vertical balls played up from opponent backs, punts, goal kicks, and free kicks from central areas of the field are the easiest to judge and head successfully. The most difficult ball defenders have to deal with is a cross from the flank that is played from close to the goal line and bending sharply toward oncoming attackers. These crosses may be hit with a lot of velocity, in addition to bending, and are extremely difficult to judge and successfully head out of danger. Often, defenders tracking an opponent forward on near-post runs actually must head the ball while running at their own goal. In general, it's easier to head the ball on defense because, in most cases, you want simply to head the ball away from your own goal. The only real technical demand is to head through the bottom half of the ball so that it goes up.

Heading to Pass the Ball

Heading as a pass to a teammate or heading to goal is much more difficult than heading defensively. Passing accurately with the head requires many of the same technical demands as passing with the feet. You have to select the correct portion of the head as a striking surface and make sure your head strikes the ball along the target line. Just as the ankle must be locked to pass or shoot the ball, the muscles of the neck must hold the head rigid and steady to pass or head to goal with power and accuracy.

HEADING DRILLS

During the drills, as players are jumping and heading, the coach will stop the exercise and make necessary observations and corrections to the group or individual players about technique.

The coach always develops exercises that become more complex and that more closely resemble what players will experience in real games. This usually means fewer numbers of players in a smaller space that graduates to a larger number of players in a larger space. Technically, the progression is from general technique without opposition in a nondirectional exercise that progresses toward functional (positional) technique in directional exercises in the appropriate third or more of the field.

When introducing heading to very young players, it's a good idea to make sure the balls are soft. Even a small beach ball or sponge ball can be used for very young players. Obviously, any youngster who really doesn't want to try heading the ball should not be forced to do so. Usually, after watching friends head for a while, the child will give it a try. Otherwise, wait until he or she is ready.

Head Juggling

Purpose: To train alone and develop technique and confidence in heading

Figure 5.7 Player stands and juggles while stationary.

Procedure: The simplest form of head juggling has the player standing and beginning stationary head juggling with a toss from the hands. As in all forms of soccer juggling, the player keeps the ball in the air with repetitive touches, in this case with the head (figure 5.7).

The player will initially keep the ball going by touches that travel only 12 to 18 inches (about 30-45 cm) above the head. In head juggling, the head will be tilted back to see the ball, and all other heading cues apply. The striking surface is the same, the eyes remain open, and the mouth stays closed. Once players are comfortable and can keep the ball going, it's time to add some juggling variations.

For starters, headers should attempt to vary the height of the juggles. They should head the ball to a height of 4 or 5 feet (1.2-1.5 m) above the head and attempt to keep it going. This is relatively difficult and will take some practice.

This drill requires very little space, and juggling can be used as a measurement tool—how many juggles can you head in a row? Players can compare their scores against teammate's totals even though they train separately.

Coaching Points: While head juggling is slightly different from game heading, juggling gives a player great feel for heading technique and confidence when heading. Juggling should be a continuous part of the player's quest for technical development. The coach should always have players perform individual juggling prior to heading with partners or functional heading practices.

Variation 1: Once players can vary the height of continuous juggling, they should try to set various rhythms. They might try two low juggles followed by one high juggle, then repeat the cadence of two low and one high as many times as they can. The variations are limited only by the players' creativity.

Variation 2: Once players are comfortable with stationary head juggling, they should practice head juggling on the move. Most soccer technique is performed while players are in motion, so once players can execute effectively while standing, they should then head on the move to mimic how players execute in real games.

Partner Heading

Purpose: To learn proper heading technique

Procedure: Two players stand 10 feet (3 m) apart and head the ball back and forth to each other. They establish a rhythm of one-touch heading with the ball describing a shallow parabola in its flight (figure 5.8). The emphasis is on striking the ball with neck muscles contracted so that the striking surface firmly contacts the ball. The eyes remain open (although they'll reflexively blink at contact) and the mouth closed.

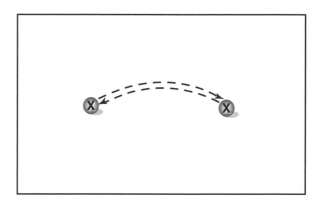

Figure 5.8   Partner Heading.

Coaching Points: Vary the distance between the players and ask them to vary the angle of heading.

Variation: To develop more feel for the ball, an alternative exercise is for the player to receive the ball with the head on the first touch and then head back to the partner on the second touch. Individual head juggling also develops the feel for the correct contact point and increased confidence in heading.

Clear or Score

Purpose: To practice defensive heading and scoring

Procedure: Two players stand on either side of a middle zone. A third player stands inside the middle zone. Cones are placed centrally to make a goal. The width of the middle zone and the size of the goals can be adjusted to meet the ability of the players. The objective is for player 1 and player 2 to head the ball over player 3 to practice defensive heading. Players 1 and 2 can also head the ball down and through the cones to practice scoring. For scoring, player 1 tosses the ball over player 3 for player 2 to head through the goal (figure 5.9). Score a point for each successful goal or defensive head. Players then rotate, and player 3 tosses for player 1.

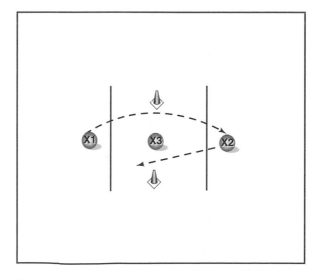

Figure 5.9   Clear or Score.

2v2 Clear or Score

Purpose: To practice defensive heading and scoring in a team setting

Procedure: This drill is similar to Clear or Score, except it's in a team format. Making the goal wider, defender 1 and defender 2 act as goalkeepers and must stay on the goal line. Attacker 1 and attacker 2 stand on either side of the middle zone. Attacker 1 tosses the ball over the defenders for attacker 2 to head down and for a goal attempt. To score, the ball must be headed below shoulder height (figure 5.10). The coach may vary the game by making the middle zone larger, increasing or decreasing the size of the goal, or restricting the defenders by not allowing them to use their hands to prevent a goal. Each team has equal time as headers. The winner can be determined by most goals in a time limitation or by total goals in a set game (e.g., first to five).

Variation: To emphasize defensive clearances using the same game, the coach may widen the middle zone or allow the defenders to move freely in the middle zone. The exercise proceeds and is scored similarly, but attacker 1 must now head the ball over the defenders and be caught by attacker 2 to count as a score. The ball may be thrown or front volleyed over the middle zone to begin the next point.

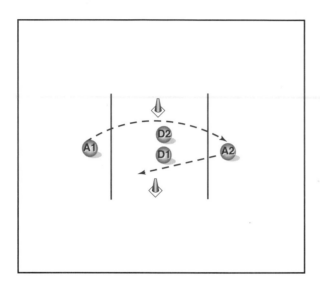

Figure 5.10 2v2 Clear or Score.

Because most heading involves jumping and contact with opponents to win head balls, the remaining drills in the chapter require players to learn and develop the explosive bow and arrow action so crucial to successful heading.

Center Circle Heading

Purpose: To improve heading technique while also practicing eye-contact signaling

Procedure: This drill includes 16 players. Eight players are distributed evenly outside the center circle, each holding a soccer ball. The other 8 players are inside the center circle (figure 5.11). The players inside the circle jog around until they make eye contact with an outside player holding a ball. On making eye contact, the inside player runs toward the outside player, and the outside player then tosses the ball for the runner to jump and head back to him or her.

Coaching Points: After each player receives many opportunities to head (and after the coach has had ample time to make corrections), the players reverse roles so that those who were inside the circle heading are now outside the circle and become the tossers.

The coach might demand a specific type of head ball. If the focus is on defensive heading, the coach might ask players to head through the bottom half of the ball to ensure that the ball goes up. The optimal angle for the defensive header is for the ball to come off the head at a 45-degree angle of flight. This causes the ball to travel the greatest distance through the air.

If heading to goal is the focus of training, the coach might ask players to head through the top half of the ball so that the ball goes down. The target for heading to goal is to try to make the ball hit the goal line, which makes for the most difficult angle for the goalkeeper to deal with.

As competency increases, the coach might demand heading to a specific target. For power, the player must head the ball as hard as possible at the tosser's chest. The ball should have a flat trajectory and be headed with power. For accuracy, the player must head the ball to someone other than the tosser. With this variation, the tosser must stay alert, but this shouldn't be a problem.

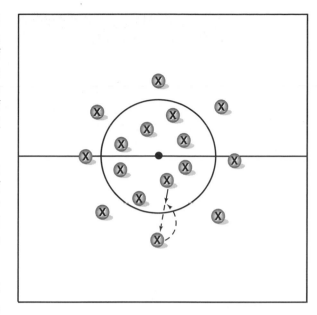

Figure 5.11　Center Circle Heading.

Rotation Heading

Purpose: To practice heading back and forth after a volley

Procedure: This drill resembles Clear or Score and 2v2 Clear or Score, but here you'll have a middle zone that's much wider than those illustrated for the previous drills. The drill involves three groups of six players (figure 5.12). Attacker 1 volleys the ball over the defenders in the middle zone to attacker 2. Attacker 2 heads the ball over the middle zone to attacker 3. Use five to seven balls to provide many opportunities for headers. If a ball drops on attacker 2's side, he or she volleys over the middle zone for attacker 1's group to head.

Coaching Points: This drill rapidly develops to both groups of attackers volleying and heading back and forth. The defenders collect missed or improperly headed balls and toss them to either side. After an appropriate time interval, one of the attacking groups exchanges with the defenders.

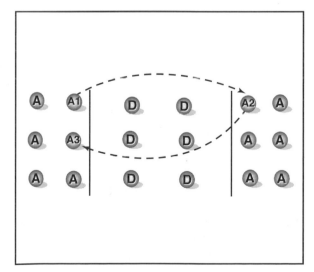

Figure 5.12　Rotation Heading.

Functional Heading

Purpose: To teach players to head to a target in a gamelike environment

Procedure: This is a three-zone drill. Two end zones are marked, 15 to 20 yards (13.7-18.2 m) long by 15 yards (13.7 m) wide. A long neutral zone connects the two end zones. The size of the three zones can be adjusted by the coach to match the skill level of players. In one end zone are three attackers. In the other end zone are three defenders. In the neutral zone is a single player. The exercise commences with a long service from the defenders into the attacking end zone. Here attacker 1 heads the ball down to the neutral player, who then passes to attacker 2 (figure 5.13a). Attacker 2 now serves to one of the defenders, who heads the ball down to the neutral player. The neutral player passes the ball back to one of the defenders, who serves to the attackers, repeating the cycle. With experienced players serving long distances, the coach may use two neutral players, one with each group of headers.

Variation 1: Figure 5.13b shows a progression from the previous drill. The size of the playing space might need to be increased for this variation. Add an attacker and defender to the opposing end zones. When defender 1 serves the ball, defender 4 tries to pressure and prevent attacker 1 from heading the ball to the neutral player. The coach can further complicate the environment by making the spaces larger and adding more headers and opponents.

Variation 2: Figure 5.13c illustrates a variation in which two neutral players play against one defender in the neutral zone. The players in the end zones must now head the ball to the open neutral player.

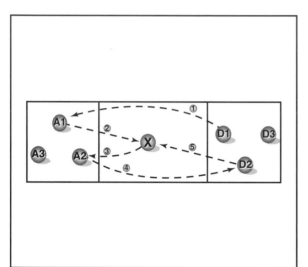

Figure 5.13a Functional Heading.

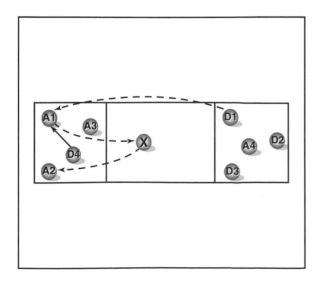

Figure 5.13b Functional Heading, variation 1.

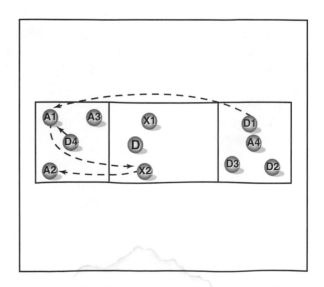

Figure 5.13c Functional Heading, variation 2.

GAMES

A training session should always culminate in a game that reflects and emphasizes what has been targeted during the session. The game may be 7v7, 9v9, or a full 11v11 game. To emphasize heading, the coach might demand that one or both teams play direct soccer. Direct soccer is playing long, high balls out of the back that bypass the midfield. Playing this way affords many opportunities for heading, both defensively and heading to goal.

Although heading does not hurt when done properly, the soccer community needs to carefully track a growing body of evidence that long-term heading might be deleterious to one's health. At the moment of impact (as the head strikes the ball), the resulting shock causes the brain to literally bounce against the inside of the cranium. Some researchers associate this impacting of the brain with possible bruising of brain tissue. With further research, the medical community will supply answers to enable us to keep soccer safe for players. For now, coaches must emphasize training of proper heading technique to minimize risk of both short- and long-term injury.

Heading has become increasingly important in today's modern, high-paced soccer. Two factors have emerged that require today's player to have more heading skill than in previous eras. Today's player is physically much more powerful. Modern fitness training methodology, made possible by quantum leaps in the understanding of muscle physiology, results in a super fit soccer player. The highly fit player covers more ground faster, which means the attacking team has less time and space in which to play the ball. The tactical answer is often to play the ball in the air over blocks of defenders, which means many more heading duels occur.

The other factor requiring more skillful heading is the organization of modern central covering systems in defense. Trying to pass or dribble the ball through this tightly packed defense is extremely difficult. The tactical result is that more attacks are occurring on the flanks, which results in many more crosses. Again, this means more heading, so both defenders and attackers must have improved heading skills to win these duels in the air.

Players and coaches need to recognize the increased demand for more skillful heading. Players must be willing to spend time on their own away from the formalized training with their coach. Coaches must devote more time during training sessions to help each player on the team become a more effective header of the ball.

Tackling

To win a soccer game, a team must score goals. Defending to keep an opponent from scoring is only part of the equation. To score goals, a team must have the ball. Tackling is not always about getting the ball away from an opponent. It can be, and often should be, about getting the ball *for* your team. Good defenders are adept at *dispossessing* attacking players of the ball, but great defenders are adept at *gaining possession of the ball* from attacking players. Techniques presented in this chapter give defenders the tools to do both.

Before much can be done with the technique of tackling, players must know how to assume a good defensive stance and an appropriate defending distance. From a good defensive stance, players can respond to an attacker's movement in the most efficient manner. A good defender is always reading and reacting to an attacker's movement, and a good defensive stance allows for the quickest reactions. Poor defensive posture or inactive feet can cost the defender the split-second required to be ready for the tackle. The opportunity to tackle is a small window, so the defender must be in position to respond as soon as an opportunity presents itself. A good defensive stance and active feet provide that readiness. To begin, the defender should be goal side (between the attacker with the ball and the goal he or she is attacking). A good defensive stance is one foot in front of the other with weight evenly distributed on the balls of the feet. The defender should be bent slightly at the waist and even more at the knees for a low center of gravity (figure 6.1). His or her feet should be constantly moving and adjusting in accordance to the movements of the offense. The staggered stance (one foot in front of the other) is meant to try to force the attacking player in a direction that will make tackling easier. The attacker is taught to attack the front foot of the defender, so the defender is constantly moving, trying to keep the front foot to one side of the attacking player.

The proper distance for defending an attacker depends in part on the position of the attacker. If the attacker is facing the defender, the defender must play off enough so as not to be beat on the dribble but close enough to take away the attacker's passing options. Once a defender has controlled the momentum of an attacking player who is facing him or her, a good rule of thumb is to maintain a distance one full arm's length away (figure 6.2). Controlling the momentum of an attacking player means that the defender has closed the space between defender and attacker and forced the attacker to slow down. Often this means that the defender and attacker are moving in the same direction at the same pace, and the defender is controlling the speed of movement. Many players defending a player running at them play too far off, assuming that if they don't get beat on the dribble they have defended successfully. However, from that distance, an attacker has the time to look up and

Figure 6.1 Good defensive stance with one foot in front of the other and a low center of gravity.

find opportunities to penetrate the defense with a pass. A single arm's length is a good starting point for the defender, and then adjustments can be made depending on the player's physical tools. A quick-footed defender with great reactions might be able to get slightly closer and still get tackling opportunities.

If circumstances are such that an attacking player possesses the ball with his or her back to the goal, the defender's priority is to keep the attacker facing that direction. The defender might move in closer now, to half an arm's length away (elbow to fingertip) from the attacker. If the attacker is facing away from the defender, the defender (especially a young defender) might tend to get too tight to the attacker, allowing the attacker to spin around the defender. The defending stance is still one foot in front of the other, but now the defender wants to maintain a stance in which his or her hips are turned in the same direction as the attacking player (figure 6.3). Again, the defender must be constantly moving, maintaining a low stance to be able to look around the attacking player to keep visual contact with the ball. Common phrases to cue defenders are *head on one side* (to peek) and *feet on the other* (to be ready to tackle).

TACKLES

Each of the many ways to get a ball away from an opponent is described here as a separate tackling technique. These include the block tackle, the poke tackle, the body tackle, and the slide tackle. All of these techniques can be used

Figure 6.2 The defender keeps the attacking player facing her and one arm's length away.

Figure 6.3 When the attacking player's back is to the goal, the defender turns her hips in the same direction of the attacking player at half of an arm's length away. The defender's head is on one side and her front foot is on the other.

in a game, but great defenders use the body tackle whenever possible and resort to the slide tackle only when no other tackle will do. Coaches must remember and appreciate that teaching defensive stance and appropriate defensive distance are critical steps in teaching any of these tackling techniques. All four types of tackle are used in games, so players must be aware of the options they have when facing an opponent who has the ball and learn to choose wisely.

Block Tackle

The block tackle is used by a defender who is challenging an attacker head on with the ability to step through the ball, such as when an attacking player is dribbling toward the attacking third. The defending player closes the space, and the team moves in defensive support. The attacking player slows as the passing options are eliminated and the space to dribble into disappears. The defender has supporting players behind him or her, the speed of the attacker is minimal, and the defender has the ability to aggressively step through the ball as the attacker looks to find an option. The critical technical aspects at play here are balance and a good body position to provide the ability to step through the tackle with the back foot. The block tackle is executed by planting solidly on the front foot, creating a stable base by getting low over that foot, and stepping through the ball with the back foot (figure 6.4a). The low stance allows the defender to come in strong, which is necessary because the attacker and defender often meet the ball at the same time. The tackling foot is toe up and heel down, which provides a large contact surface. The defender contacts the ball at the center or slightly below center (figure 6.4b). Most often, the attacker and defender are making simultaneous contact on the ball. If the defender's contact is too high on the ball, the attacking player can more easily

a

b

Figure 6.4 (a) Create a stable base and step through the ball, with the (b) toe up and heel down to contact ball a little below center.

overpower the defender and win the ball. If the defender is too low on the ball, the ball tends to roll over the tackling leg, leaving the attacking player with the ball. Advanced players might find that a slight upward motion just after contact will get the ball to roll over the contact foot of the attacker and give the defender more chance of winning the tackle.

The block tackle has three possible results—the attacker maintains possession of the ball (because of greater strength or because of improper technique by the defender); the defender wins the ball and is able to gain possession; or neither player gains possession of the ball, which leads to a new battle for possession. The defender should be prepared to quickly respond to any one of these three possibilities. If the attacker maintains possession, the defender must immediately recover and get goal side of the attacking player. If the defender had a teammate in a covering position who steps in to put pressure on the attacker who has retained possession, the original defender should recover behind that teammate and support him or her. If the defender wins possession via the tackle, the defender (now turned attacker) looks to exploit the transitional moment and pass forward or penetrate on the dribble as quickly as possible. If the tackle is successful in stripping the ball from the attacker but not in winning possession, the defender must decide if he or she has a chance to win the ball. Often, an immediate reaction to get between the loose ball and the attacker allows the defender to win the loose ball. If the loose ball is closer to an opponent, the defender must immediately prepare to defend again so that his or her team is not left vulnerable.

Poke Tackle

The aptly named poke tackle is a technique to dispossess an attacker of the ball. A poke tackle does not attempt to gain possession. In a poke tackle, the defender uses the toe of his or her front foot to reach out and poke the ball away from an attacking player (figure 6.5). The key is to maintain balance because the poke tackle is meant to be a low-risk option in which the defender does not commit him- or herself to the tackle (which risks the attacking player getting past the defender as the tackle is attempted). If the defender succeeds in getting the ball away from the attacking player's control, the next step is to try to gain possession by putting her or his body between the attacker and the ball. By winning the space around the ball, the defender can shield the attacking player from getting to the ball, gaining possession for the defender. With possession of the ball, the defender immediately transitions to attack and takes advantage of an opponent transitioning quickly to defense.

Figure 6.5 Toe reaches out and pokes the ball away from the attacking player.

Body Tackle

A body tackle is used with the goal of gaining possession from the attacking player. The technique involves the defender reading the touch of the attacker and, as the attacker takes a long touch to try to beat the defender, stepping in to put his or her body between the attacker and the ball, thereby gaining possession; the attacking player is now looking at the back of the defender who has possession of the ball. The defending player in a good defensive stance slows down the oncoming attacker with one foot in front of the other and hips turned so that the attacking player is encouraged to move in a given direction (figure 6.6a). As the attacking player takes a long touch trying to beat the defender, the defender steps with the front foot into the path of the attacker, separating the attacker from the ball (figure 6.6b). If the ball is not within playing distance of the defender, the defender can't impede the progress of the attacker, because this constitutes an obstruction foul. But if by stepping into the attacker's path, the defender can beat the attacker to the ball, the defender can legally gain possession via the body tackle (figure 6.6c). The body tackle can also be used when defending an attacking player with his or her back to the goal. As the attacking player takes a touch to attempt to turn or to move off in any direction, the defender reads the touch and wins the space around the ball by physically stepping into the space between the attacker and the ball. In a body tackle, the defender separates the attacker from the ball by finding the exact moment to step into the space created when the attacking player takes a touch away from him- or herself. Although this technique is described here as an attacking player facing a defender, the ability to see and take advantage of oppor-

a   b

Figure 6.6 (a) The defender gets in a good defensive stance with the hips turned to encourage the attacker to move in a specific direction, then as the ball is played, (b) the defender puts her body between the attacker and the ball.

Figure 6.6c The defender takes possession of the ball after the body tackle.

tunities to gain possession by positioning the body between the attacker and the ball is an important defensive skill at the higher levels of the game. Any of the other tackling techniques might result in a loose ball, whereas a body tackle is used to gain possession of the ball.

Sliding Block Tackle

First, we should say that a slide tackle should only be used when a defender can't execute any other form of tackle. A defender usually resorts to a slide tackle when an attacker has gotten past a defender and there's not enough time or space for the defender to completely recover goal side and face the attacking player he or she is attempting to defend. A slide tackle is typically executed on the flank to stop an attacker who is dribbling into dangerous areas. Because of an attacker's great speed or excellent location on the field, the defender must stop the attacker immediately to avoid a hazardous situation. The choice to leave your feet is a serious one in soccer because doing so renders you out of the game, albeit for only a short period of time. But if the tackle is not successful, your team is vulnerable during that time.

The slide tackle is essentially a block tackle, but the attacker and defender are usually running in the same direction, and the defender doesn't have the speed to get goal side and defend the player from the front. To be legal, the slide can't come from behind the attacking player, and contact must be made with the ball, not with the attacker. Rather than using the inside of the back foot, the slide tackle is done with the instep of the foot farthest from the attacker as the players run side by side (figure 6.7a). As the attacking player runs forward, the defender leaves his or her feet to extend his or her reach (figure 6.7b) and brings the far foot around to solidly meet the ball (figure 6.7c). The instep should make contact with the center to top half of the ball so that the ball doesn't roll over the foot of the defender, who is now on the ground (figure 6.7d). A block tackle has three possible results—the attacker

Figure 6.7 (a) The defender runs by the side of the attacker, (b) extends her reach, (c) brings the far foot around to meet the ball, and (d) slides to the ground and meets the ball with her foot on the top half of the ball.

maintains possession, the ball is loose, or the defender is able to win possession. By sliding, defenders put themselves in a difficult situation in which to deal with two of these possible outcomes—the ball won by the attacker or the loose ball. This is why the slide tackle should be a last resort.

Sliding Poke Tackle

The sliding poke tackle is the same as the sliding block except that the defender doesn't risk trying to win the ball and is concerned only with getting the ball away from the attacker. Either foot can be used, but often the foot nearer the attacker is extended as the defender goes to the ground, increasing his or her reach in an effort to poke the ball away. The sliding poke tackle is often used near the sidelines to poke the ball out of bounds, which strips the attacker from the ball and buys some time for the defender's team to recover and get set defensively. Again, to avoid being called for a foul, the defender must not attempt to win the ball from behind the attacking player. Even if the defender contacts the ball first, most referees will whistle for a foul if the defender goes through the legs of the attacker before or after contact is made with the ball. Slide tackling (poke or block) can also put defenders at risk of injury because their ability to control their body is lost once they leave their feet.

TACKLING DRILLS

Coaches must carefully consider activities that promote tackling because high repetition of hard tackling runs the risk of injuring players. However, it's important to provide all players opportunities to work on their individual and group defending. Players must learn to be comfortable with tackling and need to learn not only how to tackle but when to tackle.

Rock, Paper, Scissors 1v1

Purpose: To teach players to recover and get goal side to defend; to provide an environment in which many tactical decisions are necessary

Procedure: Players face each other in pairs with the ball between them and a line 10 yards (9.1 m) behind each player. To start the activity, you may use any method that quickly determines a winner between two people, such as rock, paper, scissors or a coin flip. The winner of the activity immediately takes the ball and attempts to dribble away from the other player and across a line 10 yards (9.1 m) away. The other player becomes the defender, who must get goal side and attempt to win the ball. The distance of the line can be adjusted to give the defenders more space in which to recover. You can award more points if the defender gains possession than if he or she merely pokes the ball away and keeps the attacker from getting to the line. The attacker is awarded points if he or she successfully reaches the line.

Coaching Points: Watch for proper recovery in the defender to get goal side. Also observe players' recognition of when to tackle. Note that when a defender has recovered and is facing the attacker, the defender can put more effort into the tackle with a greater chance to win the ball. Observe how well players can transition from defense to attack.

Variation: The winner of the rock, paper, scissors takes the ball and attacks forward, giving defenders repetition in defending players facing them and possibly running at them with the ball.

1v1 to a Line

Purpose: To provide repetition of defenders closing space and defending an attacker who is facing them and running at them with the ball

Procedure: Two players stand on opposite ends of a small rectangular grid with a small goal, which can be set up with cones (three yards [2.7 m] or less in width) on opposite sides of each end line (figure 6.8). The defender serves the ball across the grid to the attacking player and then steps into the grid to defend. The attacking player has three options to score—the attacker can pass through the small goal, dribble across the end line, or dribble through the small goal. The coach can assign the value of each scoring option to encourage defenders to prioritize the areas they defend. (For instance, passing through the goal scores 2 points, dribbling across the end line scores 1 point, and dribbling through the goal scores 3 points.) This encourages the defender to channel the attacker to the outside, away from the small goal (representing the center of the field), and to protect that space, especially keeping the attacker from penetrating that space with the ball. When a goal is scored or the ball goes out of bounds, the opposite player serves the ball, and players change roles. Four to six players can be assigned to each grid to provide rest between each 1v1 battle.

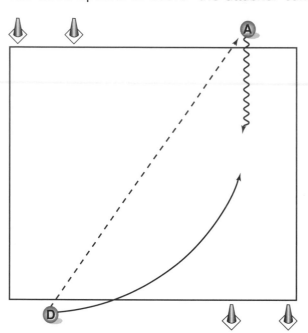

Figure 6.8 1v1 to a Line.

Coaching Points: Remind players to angle their approach to cut off the pass into the goal. Defenders should try to close the space in front of the attacker as quickly as possible while the ball is getting to the attacker, but they should slow down as the attacker touches the ball so that their own momentum is not used to the attacker's advantage (to accelerate by the defender). Watch for players immediately assuming a good defensive stance. Observe for proper tackling decisions and technique:

- If block tackling, is the weight balanced and behind the ball so that the defender has the physical advantage?
- If poke tackling, is the defender trying to win the ball or just hit the ball out of bounds and stop the attacker?
- Does the attacker provide the defender an opportunity to body tackle, giving the defender the chance to step in and win the ball?

1v1 With Servers

Purpose: To receive repetitions of 1v1 defending with an ability to read the serve into the attacker and the opportunity to win the ball before the attacker receives it

Procedure: In a small grid (about 10 by 15 yards [or 9.1 by 13.7 m]), players play 1v1, scoring when one player dribbles across the end line of the grid. Place a server for each player on either his or her defensive or attacking end. When a goal is scored or the ball goes out of bounds, a new ball is played in by the server of the attacking player. For balls that go out of bounds, the player who last touched the ball becomes the defender, and the other player's server plays a ball in to restart play. Play for one minute before players switch roles. If the server is on the defensive end, the attacker receives the ball with his or her back to the end line being attacked, and defenders get opportunities to defend players with their back to the goal. If servers are at the attacking end, they'll be serving to a player who is facing their end, and the defender will be required to defend an attacker who is facing them with the ball (figure 6.9).

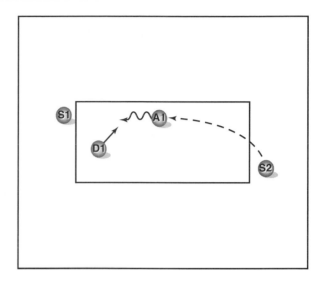

Figure 6.9 1v1 With Servers.

Coaching Points: The 1v1 defensive points are the same as in the previous drill. Watch for how well defenders can read the pass and intercept the ball. Remind players that the best defense is not allowing the player to receive the ball. Also, remind players that when defending an attacker with his or her back to the goal, the defending positioning must be slightly tighter and that the objective is to keep the attacker from turning and facing the goal.

1v1 to Targets

Purpose: To work on defending in transition and when an attacker has the option to play a teammate as well as dribble past the defender

Procedure: In a small grid (about 10 by 15 yards [or 9.1 by 13.7 m]), players play 1v1, scoring when one player receives a ball from the target on one end and plays a pass to the target on the opposite end (figure 6.10). Players always play in the same direction. This game is best played "make it, take it" because this forces defenders to play in transition. Play for one minute before players switch roles.

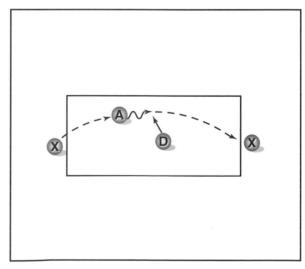

Figure 6.10 1v1 to Targets.

Coaching Points: The 1v1 defensive points are the same as in the previous drills. Observe whether defenders are close enough to the attacker to defend the pass but at a safe enough distance to prevent the attacker from taking a touch past them and beating them on the dribble.

Mark Your Own Player

Purpose: To force players to defend individually in a game setting

Procedure: Play a game with two equal teams, with each player assigned to a player on the opposite team. A player can be tackled or disposed only by the assigned player on the other team. Other players of the team may attempt to get in the way and slow down the attacker, although they are not allowed to tackle him or her (figure 6.11). (The coach may or may not allow this, depending on the skill level of the players. I would discourage it initially to force individual defenders to play good defense and to tackle correctly and at the right moment.)

Coaching Points: Individual defending points (stance and decisions) are the same as for the previous drills. In this game setting, the coach can teach the correct starting point (distance from the player being defended) prior to the ball being served. Transition is critical. The coach also watches for players' ability to defend the dribble and the pass (distance of the defender to the attacker). The decision of when to tackle now has game implications: Is the player in shooting range? Is a slide tackle necessary? Where is the danger?

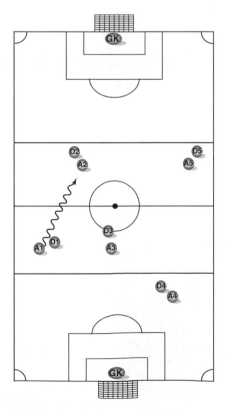

Figure 6.11 Mark Your Own Player.

Goalkeeping

There are two kinds of soccer players: goalkeepers and those wishing they could be goalkeepers. What separates the goalkeeper from the field player is the ability to use the hands to control and play the ball. The hands are primarily used to catch, parry, and box the ball. Although goalkeepers are limited to the penalty area (the rectangular box in front of the goal) as the space in which they are permitted to use their hands, this rule by no means limits where the goalkeeper can play. The goalkeeper's field of play has grown as the modern game has evolved. The elimination of using the hands to field a back pass from a teammate has forced modern goalkeepers to develop foot skills their predecessors did not require. In today's game, particularly when a goalkeeper's team is behind, you sometimes see the keeper move into the attacking third to contribute to the attack as an additional field player. The great goalkeeper Peter Schmeichel was a strong physical presence who came forward whenever Manchester United was behind in the waning minutes of a match. Jose Luis Chilavert would take free kicks well into an opponent's territory and was quite effective at this role. Today's goalkeeper has developed into a much more complete soccer player than in years past.

GETTING IN READY POSITION

Prior to making any save, a goalkeeper must first prepare to make the save. This requires the goalkeeper to get ready to move—knees are bent at a slight angle, feet are slightly wider than shoulder width apart, and hands are positioned comfortably at the sides (figure 7.1). This ready position is assumed frequently during the match. The goalkeeper must move from sprinting to ready position as quickly as possible, as demanded by circumstances during the match. Keepers who struggle to find a comfortable ready position will be less fluid in their movements and thus less effective players. As keepers become accustomed to assuming the ready position, they become quicker in their overall movements. Goalkeepers who struggle to find a good ready position will constantly find themselves either unprepared physically for play or striving to play more effectively; their movements might be awkward and ungainly as well as uncomfortable. Being caught in a position other than the ready position can result in not getting to a ball or failing to hold a ball, allowing a dangerous rebound.

Once the ready position is established and the goalkeeper decides to take action, the goalkeeper can effectively initiate movement to control or play the ball. The movements of a goalkeeper alternate from assuming the ready position, diving and catching (and so on) to save a ball, and then quickly getting back into the ready position. Very few movements of the goalkeeper are done slowly. Keepers should be sprinting between ready positions. The demands to transition from sprinting to assuming the ready position to diving and catching constantly test the athleticism of the goalkeeper during a match. Regular repetitions on the transition from sprinting to getting set (establishing ready position) are beneficial for the goalkeeper.

Figure 7.1 Set in ready position.

CATCHING BALLS

Catching the ball is a simple yet tremendously important task for a goalkeeper. By catching the ball, keepers establish possession for their team, end the opponent's attack, and begin their own team's attack. Catching a ball seems a simple task but can prove to be extremely difficult under given circumstances. Anxiety can turn the best goalkeeper's hands to stone at the wrong moment. Wet or cold weather conditions can make catching an easy ball much more difficult.

For most goalkeepers, catching requires frequent practice to reinforce skills and develop them further. The transfer of catching skills from other sports (basketball, baseball) can help develop catching skills for goalkeeping. Beginning keepers can practice catching by throwing or kicking balls against a wall and trying to catch them on the rebound. The keeper should try to catch 100 rebounds in a row with no drops, which can be challenging for keepers of all levels. As keepers become more advanced, they give themselves tougher catches until virtually every catch is automatic.

Catching Ground Balls

To catch a rolling ball or a ball below the knees requires goalkeepers to move laterally and forward so that the ball is within their body. The keeper wants to position to receive the ball between the feet and legs, within the body line (figure 7.2, a and b). Once achieving this position, the keeper keeps hands together and concentrates on catching the back and bottom of the ball (figure 7.2c).

Catching the bottom of the ball prevents the ball from skipping under the hands. Catching the sides of the ball stops the ball from sliding through the hands. Hand

a b c

Figure 7.2 (a, b) Receive ball between feet and legs. (c) Keep hands together and catch the back and bottom of the ball.

position is important, but equally important is body position and the movement required to receive the ball within the body line, which is the space between the feet (when comfortably spread) up through the shoulders. Goalkeepers should always move to receive the ball within the body line. They need to be in position to catch the ball with hands directly in front of the body, not to the side or outside the body line. To move, either a shuffle or sprint is recommended. Shuffling allows for adjustments to be made during pursuit of the ball and helps maintain balance. Obviously, sprinting makes for quicker movement to the ball. Advanced goalkeepers can sprint to a ball and rapidly compose themselves physically as they prepare to catch. At the moment of the catch, the body movement should be controlled and steady. Movement during a catch can lead to bobbling the ball and losing possession. Remaining steady provides the safest catching environment.

Catching Air Balls

Catching air balls presents a challenge different from catching balls close to or on the ground. Judging ball flight, including the spin and pace of the ball, is difficult for even the most experienced goalkeeper. Catching ground balls can be good practice for catching balls in the air. Generally, the progression is to become adept at catching ground balls, then move on to catching air balls. Once catching skills have been established, the ability to judge the flight of a ball is paramount. To judge a ball's flight once it is struck is an ability that requires much experience. Goalkeepers must take thousands of repetitions because no two balls will have exactly the same combination of factors at play in influencing the flight of the ball.

Between Knees and Abdomen Balls coming between the knees and the abdomen should be taken within the body line with hands and arms positioned similarly to when receiving a low ball. When catching balls between the thigh and the abdomen, the forearms should stay parallel and the hands together (figure 7.3a).

The upper body is concaved over the ball. The ball should be received on the forearms with the hands extended. On receiving the ball, the forearms curl up and secure the ball to the chest. Hands are tucked under the chin, and forearms remain parallel (figure 7.3b).

a   b

Figure 7.3 *(a)* Forearms stay parallel and hands stay together. *(b)* Create a concave body position, curling the forearms up and tucking the hands under the chin.

Between Abdomen and Chest In preparing to catch a ball between the abdomen and the chest, the goalkeeper must decide whether to catch with the hands pointing upward or pointing downward. This decision can be difficult, and many repetitions are needed to help make the decision automatic and the goalkeeper confident in decision making.

When the ball is received at chest level or above, hand position is extremely important. Hands should be extended upward (figure 7.4a), with thumbs close together and hands contoured to the shape of the ball. Wrists should be bent slightly forward. The goalkeeper should try to catch the top and back of the ball (figure 7.4b). Catching the top of the ball prevents the ball from skipping off and over the hands. With this method, if the ball is not held, it should drop in front of the keeper, allowing a quick recovery of the ball outside the goal. Catching the back of the ball also prevents the ball from slipping through the hands. Elbows should remain comfortably close, because pulling the elbows apart forces the thumbs apart. Catching balls between the abdomen and chest is largely an intuitive task that requires many repetitions. Every goalkeeper needs to catch balls at this height every session.

a

b

Figure 7.4 *(a)* Extend hands upward and *(b)* catch the top and back of the ball.

High-Flighted Balls Because of the timing of the jump, pace of the ball, and opponent pressure, high-flighted balls are often the most challenging balls to catch. As with balls at chest level, the goalkeeper should attempt to catch the back and top of the ball. Arms should be angled slightly forward, allowing the goalkeeper to sight the ball all the way into the hands and provide strength to possess the ball (figure 7.5a). If required to jump to catch the ball, the goalkeeper should jump forward, usually in the direction of the flight of the ball. Jumping forward off one foot permits the keeper to jump higher and attack the ball (figure 7.5b).

This forward motion also allows the goalkeeper to be strong and withstand challenges from opponents. A simple drill for this technique is to position the keeper on one side of a line facing the line. The coach tosses the ball at various heights above the line. The keeper works on timing the run up to the ball and the jump so that he or she leaves from one side of the line, catches the ball above the line, and lands on the other side of the line. The coach is looking for the keeper to receive the ball as high as possible, with arms slightly forward.

The progression is for the coach to toss the ball straight above the line and over the coach's head. To present a physical challenge to the keeper, the coach should push the upper body of the keeper. The keeper needs to maintain focus on the ball despite the physical challenge and to jump lifting the leg closest to the challenge to keep the opponent (coach) away from the keeper's body.

a   b

Figure 7.5 (a) Angle the arms slightly forward. (b) Jump off one foot to attack the ball.

BOXING AND PARRYING

When goalkeepers feel they aren't able to hold an incoming ball, the options are to box (punch) or parry the ball. Parrying is most often used on shots that can't be held. Boxing is generally used for balls flighted into the keeper's area.

Parrying is performed with one or both hands (most frequently with one hand to shots wide of the goalkeeper's body). The firm base of the palm is the preferred surface for parrying because it provides the strength to parry the ball well away from the goal area (figure 7.6).

Figure 7.6 Use the base of the palm for the best strength.

In some cases, such as when a ball is extremely wide, keepers must use their fingers to parry because only their fingers can reach the ball. In any case, the keeper should extend the arm at a slightly forward angle and time this arm extension to drive the ball away from the goal. In wet conditions, a parry is often the best choice. When the ball is coming extra fast and there's not much time to react, or when opponent traffic is heavy in front of the goalkeeper, a parry is usually much safer than trying a catch. Catching has its rewards (no rebounds, maintains possession for the team, and so on), but often the risks outweigh the rewards.

Boxing the ball requires striking the ball with the flat surface of the fist. When boxing a flighted ball falling in front of the goalkeeper, it is preferable to use two fists together to form one large flat surface (figure 7.7).

Fists should start at the chest and drive forward, striking the bottom of the ball. The aim of the goalkeeper is to drive the ball high, far, and wide, in that order of priority. Driving the ball high allows the keeper either a second attempt at holding the ball or time to recover and reposition. Driving the ball far makes a second chance for the opponent difficult and also buys time for the defense and keeper to recover. A wide drive provides a more difficult finishing angle for the opponent.

Balls flighted beyond the goalkeeper (e.g., back post) should be handled with one fist. The same flat surface is used but with a different motion, similar to a jab in which the fist starts at the chest and drives through the bottom of the ball (figure 7.8). The ball will then carry farther and higher, missing its intended target and playing safely wide. Avoid a windmill (round arcing) motion. A straight-line motion presents a better chance at contact and results in a better redirection.

Figure 7.7 Use two fists together to box a flighted ball in front of the goalkeeper.

Figure 7.8 Drive through the bottom of the ball.

DIVING

For balls struck in such a way that goalkeepers can't field the ball within their body line, they must dive to save the ball. In such cases, several considerations are necessary. Catching a ball when diving is similar to catching a high ball. Arms are slightly forward of the body, and the catch is made at the back and top of the ball. Parrying is frequently performed while diving and may be done with one or two hands. Parrying is generally the preferred technique or choice when the goalkeeper is not sure that the ball can be held during a dive.

Footwork and foot speed are crucial for a successful dive. The goalkeeper must move as quickly as possible toward the ball. The last stride before beginning the dive should be long because this positions the keeper closer to the ball and increases the speed and force at which he or she can dive (figure 7.9a). When diving, the keeper should leave from the foot closer to the ball (e.g., for a ball to the right, the keeper leaves from the right foot; see figure 7.9b). Hands move directly to the ball with the head almost between the arms—this prevents the keeper from directly reaching across the body and provides the best situation for the hands to catch the ball.

a

b

Figure 7.9 (a) The last stride is long toward the ball, and (b) the arms move directly toward the ball with head between them.

If the ball is held, the ball should contact the ground before the upper body (figure 7.10a). This reduces the landing impact for the body and provides a safe contact option for the ball. The ground provides a stable place to situate the ball. The arms should absorb any further impact forces. The body should finish behind the ball between the ball and the goal (figure 7.10b). If the ball is parried, the goalkeeper should land on his or her side (figure 7.11).

A good exercise for teaching and reinforcing good diving technique is for the coach and goalkeeper to be positioned face to face about a yard (.9 m) apart. The coach holds the ball in one hand with the arm extended out. The goalkeeper strides for-

a

b

Figure 7.10 When landing with the ball, *(a)* contact the ground with the ball before the upper body and *(b)* finish between the ball and the goal.

ward, making sure the foot is placed under the ball and the coach's hand, takes the ball, and places it on the ground in a forward motion. The ball should finish beyond a line extending along the arm of the coach. The finishing position should be with the ball and upper portion of the goalkeeper beyond the coach. Be sure to reinforce the long stride so that the goalkeeper is landing under control with the ball striking the ground first.

To build on this drill, the coach and goalkeeper begin as before. The coach holds the ball in his or her hands and tosses it to one side. The keeper dives to catch the ball, making sure to dive at a forward

Figure 7.11 Land on the side after a parry.

angle, which should result in the keeper being even with or beyond the coach. During the dive, the keeper may or may not have both feet leave the ground. The foot toward the ball should be taking a long stride to the ball and then may stay on the ground until after the completion of the dive. The coach then backpedals and receives the ball back from the keeper. The keeper stands, and the coach tosses the ball to the opposite side. The keeper should be forcing the coach to backpedal with each dive forward. This drill is a good teaching tool and can be used for warming up an advanced goalkeeper. As the keeper begins to master the task, the speed at which the coach demands the keeper to recover and make the next save increases, providing more pressure and conditioning.

POSITIONING

Proper positioning can prevent as many goals as accurate diving can. Usually, the goalkeeper should be on a line between the ball and the center of the goal. This line is called the *ball line* (figure 7.12a). Such positioning ensures that the goalkeeper is equidistant from shots to either post. How far out along the ball line the goalkeeper should position depends on several factors, including game situation; goalkeeper's level of experience; goalkeeper's size, speed, and vertical jumping ability; and the abilities and tendencies of the opponent.

The goalkeeper can cut the angle of the shooter by moving out along the ball line. This movement reduces the distance between the goalkeeper and a shot at either post. In figure 7.12b, a goalkeeper at position 1 has farther to travel to intercept a shot to either post than does a goalkeeper at position 2. However, moving out along the ball line makes the keeper more vulnerable to a ball played over his or her head. With experience, each goalkeeper will find his or her own optimal spot along the ball line for each given situation. Generally, keepers are conservative in playing close to the goal line and should be encouraged to position more aggressively, such as closer to the ball or farther out on the ball line.

There are several situations in which a goalkeeper is not on the ball line. For instance, balls played from the flanks require a keeper to consider the most likely play by the opponent with the ball and to position accordingly. If the ball is most likely to be swerved to the top of the six-yard box, the keeper may stray from the ball line. Of course, the keeper must remember that the first priority is to protect the goal. A keeper who has anticipated a ball flighted near the six-yard line and positioned for such a ball should be wary—keepers at every level have been caught out of position for a ball struck (intentionally or unintentionally) directly at the goal.

Positioning for flighted balls depends on the ability of the server, ability of the goalkeeper, and a variety of other factors (size of field, weather conditions, and so on). General guidelines for the goalkeeper defending balls on the flank are to play off the line as far as possible without compromising his or her ability to save shots on goal. If the server is under pressure, the keeper should play toward the near post because the serve will likely be short. If the server is unpressured, the keeper should position more centrally. The optimal position depends on many factors and is best learned through repeatedly placing the keeper in situations with opponents wide with the ball. Channel games—small-sided teams playing centrally with free players in wide channels—can provide great learning environments.

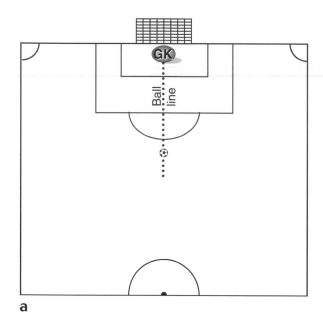

a

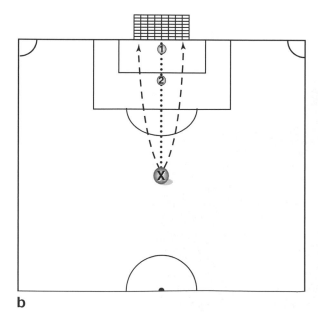

b

Figure 7.12 *(a)* The ball line. *(b)* Positioning along the ball line.

DEFENDING BREAKAWAYS

A breakaway situation can occur whenever goalkeepers find themselves alone against an opponent. This might be seen when a long ball is played behind the defense to an attacking forward, or when a defender slips as an attacker closes in on goal. In both cases the goalkeeper is called on to make a breakaway save, which requires the keeper to attack the ball. This is done best by advancing to the ball between the opponent's touches. While the opponent is capable of shooting the ball, the keeper must be ready to defend the shot and assume the ready position. The breakaway technique is similar to saving a low ball. The keeper leads with the hands and takes the fastest path to the ball. By leading with the hands all the way to the ball, the hands and arms protect the head (figure 7.13a).

It is important for the goalkeeper to go down on the side of the body corresponding to which side the ball is on (e.g., if the ball is on the goalkeeper's left, the keeper should go down on the left side of the body, figure 7.13b). A simple exercise for

a

b

Figure 7.13 *(a)* Lead with hands and take most direct path to the ball. *(b)* Go down on side of the body to receive the ball.

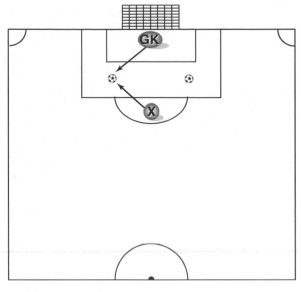

Figure 7.14 Exercise to teach breakaway technique.

teaching this technique is for a field player to start on the arc outside the penalty area with two balls placed 4 yards (~3.6 m) on each side of the penalty spot (figure 7.14).

Communication is essential for the goalkeeper, especially during breakaway and flighted ball situations. A goalkeeper should declare his or her intentions and directives to teammates early and clearly. "Keeper" lets teammates know the goalkeeper is attempting to win the ball. "Away" means the goalkeeper is not coming for the ball and teammates should play the ball away. Organization of the defense relies on effective communication. Key to effective communication and instruction is using names ("Mark number 8, Jackie") rather than general instruction ("Mark number 8" or "Everyone mark up!"). Avoiding unnecessary words increases the impact of directions made in crucial situations. Short, direct commands work best.

DISTRIBUTING THE BALL

Once the goalkeeper wins the ball, the attack starts from the goalkeeper. Goalkeeper distribution is done either with the foot (kick, volley, or half-volley) or hand (roll, baseball throw, or sling throw). The goalkeeper must possess good kicking skills for clearing the ball as well as passing and possessing the ball. Teams with a strong-footed goalkeeper enjoy an extra option in the back.

The kicking skills for a goalkeeper are the same as for any other defender. The emphasis is on striking a long ball with accuracy. Keepers should be able to clear a ball with either foot. The first concern of the keeper is safety, followed by distance, height, and accuracy.

A goalkeeper should be responsible for taking goal kicks. Taking goal kicks requires patience and practice, but the payoff is important for the team. Goalkeepers should be taking goal kicks at an early age to work on the skill as well as the choices involved when taking a goal kick.

The volley, or punt, requires the goalkeeper to drop the ball and strike it before it hits the ground. This method is valued for distance but has a very long hang time (the time the ball is in the air), aiding the opponent. The goalkeeper should make sure to drop the ball in front and run through the motion. The ball should have backspin as it travels to its intended target.

A half-volley is when the ball is dropped by the goalkeeper and struck immediately after striking the ground. This choice of distribution aids in counterattacks because the ball travels a lower trajectory than a volley and thus arrives more quickly to its target. The downside is that a half-volley can be less consistent than a volley and thus yield varying results.

Distribution by rolling the ball is effective because the ball is easily controlled by the recipient. The disadvantages are limited distance and slow pace. The field player receiving the ball must be close to the goalkeeper and have a large amount of space to play into.

A baseball throw is exactly that—the keeper throws the soccer ball as if it were a baseball (figure 7.15). This results in a faster distribution over a greater distance than a roll, yet the ball is still easily controlled, especially when thrown so that it bounces before reaching its target. This throw requires a line clear of opponents between the goalkeeper and recipient. Baseball throws are highly effective and used very frequently. Younger keepers might struggle with this technique because their hands aren't big enough to cradle the ball as necessary. For these players, the ball might slip out of the hands during the preliminary motion.

The sling throw is difficult to master yet offers several benefits. This technique requires the ball to be cupped in the hand and supported by a bent wrist (figure 7.16a). The throwing arm is stiff, and the elbow doesn't bend throughout the motion. The arm starts at the side of the body and swings in a large arc (clockwise for right-handers) back to front (figure 7.16b). The ball is released just after the top of the arc, resulting in a long throw with a high trajectory. The ball should have a

Figure 7.15 Cradle the ball and throw like a baseball.

a   b

Figure 7.16 (a) Cup ball and support with a bent wrist. (b) Start from side of body and swing clockwise in an arced motion.

good amount of backspin. The keeper should make sure the arm swings straight overhead, with the arm brushing past the ear, which produces backspin rather than sidespin. The backspin makes the ball easy to control for the receiver, whereas the lofting arc allows the goalkeeper to throw over opposing players. Thus, a clear line between the goalkeeper and receiver is not necessary. The ability to throw over opponents and cover long distances makes the sling throw an effective method for distributing the ball. The skill is difficult to master but worth the effort.

UNDERSTANDING GOALKEEPER MENTALITY

If you ask forwards to name their five most memorable moments on a soccer field, they'll almost certainly cite their personal list of great goals and 1v1 victories. On the other hand, if you ask goalkeepers for *their* list of most memorable moments, you'll likely hear a litany of dropped balls, wrong decisions, bad luck, and the occasional save.

The psychology of goalkeepers is unlike the psychology of field players. Goalkeepers are used to receiving very little attention—in games or in training. They are often considered tools for training field players. Add to this the fact that goalkeepers are usually either great heroes or great goats (and seldom in between) and you'll begin to understand why keepers have a (sometimes well-deserved) reputation for being odd.

The physical and psychological demands of goalkeeping are infrequent bursts of maximum effort and focus. Whereas a field player might choose to rest rather than make a run, rationalizing that some rest will allow better performance later on, the goalkeeper has no such luxury of choice. Because of the demands of their position, keepers should train at high levels of intensity. They might not be involved in every drill or exercise, but when they are involved they should train with maximum effort to simulate gamelike conditions.

Goalkeepers can be very hard on themselves. After a bad game, keepers often come early and stay late for extra training. The keeper wants to earn the right to start the next game. Because goalkeeper training is very individualized, any time extra training can reasonably be accommodated it will reap benefits for both the keeper and the team.

GOALKEEPING DRILLS

A coach will seldom find a player more appreciative of individual attention than a goalkeeper is. Because keepers are accustomed to participating in training that focuses on the skills of attacking players, they love occasional drills customized just for them. Here are some drills that focus on sharpening goalkeeper skills.

Channel Games

Purpose: To practice positioning on flighted balls

Procedure: Two neutral players (X) are the only players allowed in the channels (figure 7.17). Two teams play in the central channel. The neutral players play to whichever team plays them the ball. They might have limited time or touches. To encourage crossing, additional points may be awarded for scoring off a crossed ball from a neutral player.

Coaching Points: Focus on goalkeepers correctly positioning for the cross (off the ball line), fielding crossed balls, and quickly adjusting to a change in position (off the ball line for a cross to on the ball line to stop a shot).

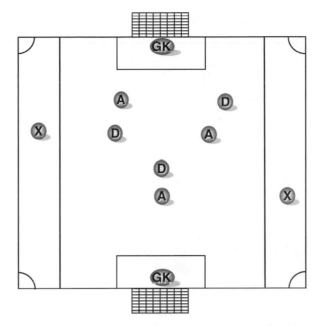

Figure 7.17 Channel Games.

Body Line

Purpose: To teach and reinforce the idea of getting the ball within the body line

Procedure: Have a coach with a ball positioned about 10 yards (9.1 m) away from the goalkeeper (figure 7.18). The keeper places a cone 1 yard (.9 m) in front of himself or herself. The coach rolls a ball wide of the reference point, and the keeper moves to receive the ball within the body line and in front of the line of the reference point. The keeper must attack the ball to receive the ball in front of the line. The coach then allows the keeper to return behind the reference point before rolling the ball on the opposite side.

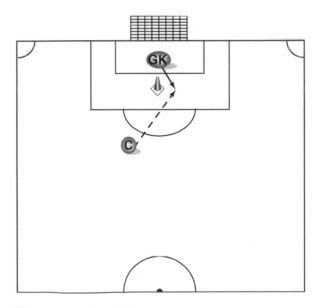

Figure 7.18 Body Line.

Coaching Points: Look for the goalkeeper to move wide so that the ball is received within the body line. A good indicator is having one foot outside the ball (if the ball is to the keeper's right, the right foot is wide of the ball). The wide foot should be higher (closer to the coach), so the keeper is turned slightly to face the direction in which the ball has traveled.

Cut Off the Angle

Purpose: To practice cutting off the angle of the attacker

Procedure: The keeper is on the opposite side starting on the six-yard line. When the field player moves to one of the balls, the keeper reacts and makes a breakaway save on the ball. When the keeper can win the ball, he or she should go down and win possession. If the field player can maintain possession, the keeper cuts the angle by advancing toward the field player and waiting for the next opportunity (e.g., a long touch) to win the ball. When the field player gets to the ball first, the field player tries to score.

Coaching Points: Watch for quick decisions from the keeper. Once the decision has been made, the keeper needs to move quickly, without hesitation, to win the ball. Watch for leading with the hands when going for the ball.

Breakaway

Purpose: To practice defending more advanced breakaways

Procedure: A higher-level exercise involving breakaways is for the goalkeeper to start on the goal line in the middle of the goal. The field player starts with a foot on the ball and the ball on the intersection of the six-yard box and the end line. Once the field player moves into the field, the goalkeeper can move to try to stop the field player from scoring. The field player's objective is to score. Play is live. If appropriate, place a time limit on the field player.

Coaching Points: The keeper must quickly advance to the ball line to protect the goal while seeking an opportune moment (e.g., bad touch) to win the ball.

Applying Techniques Tactically

Technique is learned from simple to complex. Young players make short, simple passes, and as they get older these passes become longer and more complex. Acquisition of technique also proceeds from general to specific. A child kicking a ball with an older sibling or parent simply kicks the ball in the general direction of the parent with no concern for how hard or high the ball is kicked or if it needs to be curved. As children become older, they learn that the ball can be kicked through the air to the target or can be kicked with greater velocity. By using different surfaces of the foot and by striking the ball slightly off center, they acquire the ability to bend the ball. The technique of kicking the ball becomes more complex and specific. Youngsters also must acquire the ability to pass to a moving target, a much more complex technical challenge than passing to a stationary target. Considerations of where to pass the ball and how hard to strike it now involve leading a running target with the correct passing angle and velocity to intersect the runner. New problems emerge when players must play the ball over a defender or bend the ball around a defender and into the path of a running teammate. The technical demands of soccer become increasingly complex as they require more specificity in their execution.

The development of a soccer player who can play technically at speed and execute technically in a dynamic tactical environment is a complex, involved process that takes many years. Soccer is a *late specialization* sport. Soccer players do not mature into complete players until well into adulthood. The optimal age of today's professional player is 28 or 29 years, and older for goalkeepers. In contrast, a sport like gymnastics is an *early specialization* sport. Some of the most successful gymnasts peak in the early to midteen years.

Player development is a process that proceeds in direct proportion to the time spent experiencing the four components of the game: technique, tactics, fitness, and psychology. For the youngest players, those from 6 to 12 years, the soccer experience must be about technique and the 1v1 duel. Practice sessions should be devoted to developing soccer skill through technical training and 1v1 play. Games for these players should be age appropriate in terms of the number of players and the size of the field. Ten-year-olds, for example, should play on a field 50 to 60 yards (~45-54 m) long by 30 to 35 yards (~27-32 m) wide, and they should play 6v6. The number of players and size of field should ensure that all players will have plenty of ball contact to aid technical development and should ensure that all players will be able to *find the game*—meaning there will be many opportunities to shoot and score goals. When all players have a chance to dribble, pass, score goals, and so on, the fun quotient is quite high.

As physical and psychological maturation occurs, tactical play is introduced. It is important to understand that without the ability to play technically, tactics are limited to only the most primitive. An extensive and sophisticated range of technique possessed by the player expands the tactical options available.

Technical development is an ongoing, evolving process. Players must spend many hours practicing technique away from the formal practice session. As players become older, formal practice sessions often don't allow time for specific technique practice. It is here that the commitment to improve must emerge in the motivated player. The athlete who makes it is the one who works hardest when no one else is watching.

RECOGNIZING TECHNICAL DEMANDS BY AGE

Technical demands are determined by the tactical situation. For example, an experienced flank player crossing the ball must have the technical competency to find very specific targets. He or she must have an early cross, a driven cross to the near-post space, a partially driven-chipped cross to the back-post space, and a cross driven through the second six-yard box. The tactical situation will determine which cross the flank player chooses. The cross to each of these spaces is a very specific cross that must arrive in that space with specific parameters of spin (which determines curve), velocity, and height.

The acquisition process for crossing begins with young players at about 12 years of age. The technical demand is a very general one. The coach simply asks the player if he or she can cross the ball in the air into the box in front of the goal. This is a very general target that players of this age group can typically execute.

When the player becomes a little older (12 to 13 years old), the coach now asks him or her not only to cross the ball in the air but also to bend the ball away from the goalkeeper so the goalkeeper can't cut out the cross. If the keeper cuts out the cross, it's like any other defender intercepting a pass. The keeper can now use a drop kick to launch a counterattack or throw to an open teammate to begin an attack. The technical demand for the cross must implement the first tactical objective of any cross into the box—to eliminate the goalkeeper. This cross is slightly more specific than just a ball crossed into the middle of the box.

During the ages of 14 to 15 years old our player must acquire the technical ability to hit a driven ball across the second six-yard box. This is a ball struck very hard about chest or head high that is bending away from the goalkeeper as it passes through the second six. The cross has now become more specific.

As the midteen years approach, the tactical demands for the cross increase as the complexity and sophistication of collective defending at the last line of retreat require even more specific crosses.

The near- and far-post spaces become targets for the crosser. The ball crossed into the near-post space is struck very hard, as one would in shooting the ball. The near-post cross must be struck very hard because the attacker sprinting into the near-post space redirects the ball into the goal. If the cross arrives below the waist, the attacker will lock his or her ankle and use the velocity of the cross to redirect the ball toward the goal. If the ball is above the waist, the attacker will use the velocity of the cross to redirect the ball toward the goal with a dive header. Further, because the near-post space is close to the goalkeeper, the cross must be struck very hard to prevent the keeper from coming out and intercepting the cross. The far-post cross is a delicate ball that is partially driven and chipped that goes above and just beyond the keeper. The cross needs only to clear the keeper because the far-post space is far enough away from the keeper's initial position that he or she cannot turn and get to it.

As a flank player approaches the goal line and forwards bend to the side away from the ball, some defenders pressure the ball while others track the forwards. This empties a space at the top of the box for a ball pulled back by our flank player as he or she is arriving at the goal line. The flank player must be able to pull the ball diagonally back into the space at the top of the box.

Finally, the tactical situation might present an opportunity for an early cross, which is a ball driven from wide areas behind a line of retreating defenders but in front of the goalkeeper. This ball must be driven hard, chest to head high, and must be bending sharply away from the goalkeeper as it clears the line of defenders. The early cross has become a much more valuable cross with the recent tactical emphasis of zonal defending. A zonal defense is flatter or more square than a defense with a sweeper standing behind a line of markers. With a flatter defensive block, more space is available between the goalkeeper and the defenders into which early crosses can be played.

TACTICAL APPLICATION OF CROSSING

The acquisition process for the technique of crossing proceeds from general to specific. When players are children, we give them very general, age-appropriate technical tasks. As they mature, become stronger, and devote more time to training—and as tactical demands become more complex—the crossing technique must become very specific.

The crosser's task is to strike a quality cross into one of the attacking spaces. It's the responsibility of the runners to time their runs so that one of them arrives in the space at the instant the ball arrives. The most difficult run to time is to the near post. The run must be a full sprint to get a step on the marker. If the run is too early, the runner will have to slow up and wait for the ball, allowing the marker to catch up. If the run is too late, the ball will be through the space before that runner arrives. The back-post runner will bend his or her run and hold it until he or she reads the flight of the ball. When making runs in the box against good, tight marking defenders, attackers must get across the face of these defenders.

Crossing to Second Six-Yard Box

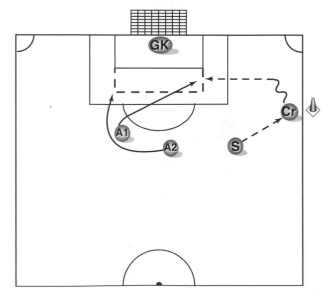

Figure 8.1 Crossing to Second Six-Yard Box.

Purpose: To develop crossing skills in all players

Procedure: In figure 8.1, the crosser (Cr) will receive a rolling ball from the server (S). The crosser crosses to the second six-yard box as attackers 1 and 2 make runs through it. The first (near-post) runner is the player farthest from the ball or the highest forward (attacker 1). Attacker 2 holds his or her run to arrive in the second six a fraction later and diagonally behind attacker 1. This gives depth to the runners so that if the cross is behind attacker 1, attacker 2 will be positioned to finish the cross. All players should perform this exercise because the dynamic nature of soccer demands that even backs may end up crossing or even getting on the end of crosses. This exercise should be done from both flanks.

Crossing to Near- and Far-Post Spaces

Purpose: To practice quality strikes to near-post and far-post spaces

Procedure: Figure 8.2 becomes more specific for the crosser, as a near-post space and a far-post space are marked on the field (in addition to the second six). The coach may use cones or vests to make a visual representation of the general size and location of the respective spaces. The diagram shows the relative location and size of the near- and far-post spaces. The far-post space is larger and located diagonally behind the near-post space (depth). The crosser will dribble the ball diagonally from the touchline cones toward the goal-line cone. As the crosser nears the goal line, he or she makes a long preparation prior to striking the cross. Attackers 1 and 2 make their runs and read the body language and position of the crosser to know when to arrive in their respective spaces. Timing of the runs is essential.

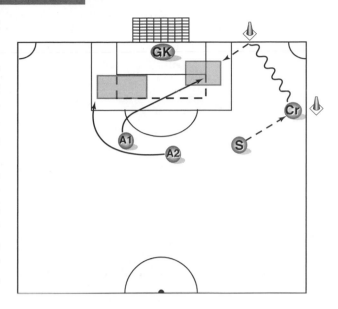

Figure 8.2 Crossing to Near- and Far-Post Spaces.

Coaching Points: The attackers must time their runs so that they arrive in the near or far post space at the same time as the ball. Split-second timing will give an attacker the advantage of being a step ahead of the defender. This exercise should be done from both flanks.

Crossing to Four Attacking Spaces in Box

Purpose: To practice quality crosses into all attacking spaces in the box

Procedure: Figure 8.3a shows the same organization as figure 8.2, but now the space at the top of the box is added so that the crosser has four possible crosses to execute: near post, back post, second six, or top of the box. Attacker 3 is usually a midfield player who will leave the space alive by staying deep until he or she sees the ball being pulled back. Like the other runners, the midfield player wants to arrive in the space at the instant the ball arrives.

Variation: Once the players are familiar enough with the types for services, spaces, and timing of runs, the coach will add defenders 1 and 2. The coach initially asks defenders to find a player early and mark that player. With three runners, one will be free, and the crosser tries to hit that

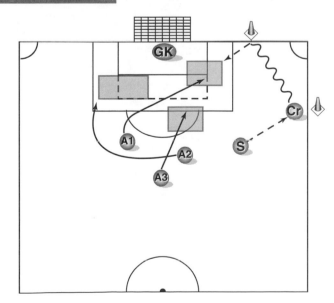

Figure 8.3a Crossing to Four Attacking Spaces in Box.

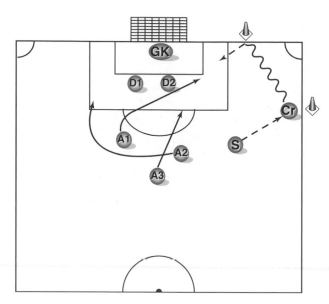

Figure 8.3b Crossing to Four Attacking Spaces in Box variation.

space. The crosser has no concern with trying to time the runner. The crosser's role is to hit the correct type of cross to the appropriate space. The runner must time a run to arrive in the space at the same instant the ball arrives (figure 8.3b).

Coaching Points: To beat a defender, the attacker should drive to run behind his or her defender, and when the defender opens his or her shoulder to turn, the attacker will cut across the defender's face before the defender can turn back to chase the attacker. The defender opening his or her shoulder is the signal for the attacker to sprint to the ball. The coach must be very flexible to ensure that players are experiencing some success. This might mean using only one defender or adding a fourth runner who will time a run to arrive in the midgoal area of the second six.

Crossing With a Neutral Zone

Purpose: To give crossers repeated repetitions at choosing and striking the cross correctly

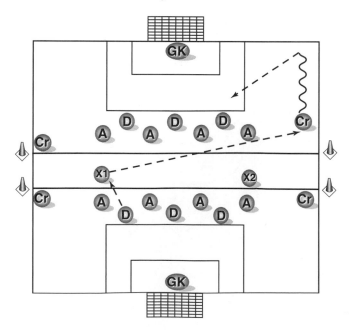

Figure 8.4 Crossing With a Neutral Zone.

Procedure: Four attackers play versus three defenders at either end of half a field. A small neutral zone is created containing two neutral players. All players must stay in their respective zones. The attackers are playing 4v3 in each final third. When a defender or the goalkeeper wins possession, he or she plays to the closest neutral player, who then must play a diagonal pass to the opposite crosser, who dribbles and then crosses to the appropriate space (figure 8.4). The use of the neutral player and the diagonal pass allows time for the attacking group to organize their runs.

Coaching Points: Always, when crossers are unsure of which space to play to, they should hit the head-high, driven cross through the second six-yard box space. That cross should find one of the runners.

TACTICAL APPLICATION OF HEADING

A critical tactical application of heading is the clearing of crosses, free kicks and corners, or any high ball played into the box. Players must learn to head the ball cleanly and powerfully in the crowded confines of the penalty box.

Heading exercises for youths are structured to overcome the fear of heading and differentiating defensive heading from heading to targets or the goal. As players mature, they gravitate to playing positions or fulfilling tactical roles, and heading becomes tactical. Forwards head to goal, and central defenders clear defensive headers. The tactical application of heading technique is clearly a function of positional responsibility. It's interesting to note that these responsibilities may be reversed in the case of restarts. A tall forward known to be able to score goals with headers may be asked to come back into the box to head defensively when the opponent has a corner or free kick. Likewise, a tall central defender whose major tactical responsibility is to head defensively in his or her own box is often asked to go forward and try to get on the end of back-post corners and head to goal.

Coaches should understand that whenever they're designing a technical training exercise, the objective is to provide players with many repetitions at the targeted technique or subtechnique. The construction of a tactical training exercise, however, should provide players with many repetitions at decision making from the possible tactical options. A central defender often has to make a decision to simply clear the ball with a powerful header to get it out of danger or head it down to a teammate, which will ensure possession for his or her team.

The tactical training exercise will always necessitate correct technical execution, no matter what tactical option is selected.

Note that whenever the coach designs an exercise, the objective is to alter a playing behavior. The exercise objective might target individual player behavior (become a better header), block behavior (how the midfield block defends), team behavior (the blocks moving together as a unit), or combinations of the three.

It's important that players remember the tactics of winning head balls. When trying to win an individual heading duel, the header must first get into the line of flight of the ball. Whenever possible, the header should time the jump to be able to take a step or two forward when attacking the ball so that the jump can begin from a one-foot takeoff. The momentum of a couple steps and a one-foot takeoff permits a higher jump by the header. A critical factor in winning the ball is for the header to jump first and spread the arms out with elbows flexed; now the header will form a cone of space around him- or herself. This cone wards off attempts by opponents to get to the ball.

Central Defender Clearances

Purpose: To train central defenders to head clearances out of their box

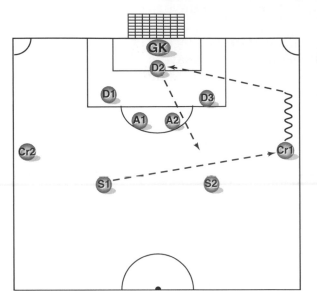

Figure 8.5 Central Defender Clearances.

Procedure: Three defenders line up along the top of the box. Crossers 1 and 2 play wide at the flanks and are served balls to cross into the box for the defenders to clear. Servers 1 and 2 are midfield players about 30 yards (27 m) from goal. The goalkeeper has a large supply of balls in the goal. This is a continuous exercise that begins with a midfield server playing a ball to the opposite crosser. The crosser dribbles and crosses the ball from various positions along the flank. Defenders head the ball out toward the midfield servers (figure 8.5). As soon as a server receives the header, he or she serves the opposite crosser, and the exercise continues. The coach may begin without attacking opposition and add one or both as the exercise develops (attackers 1 and 2 in figure 8.5).

Coaching Points: If a ball is misheaded or the header heads a ball the midfielder can't get, the goalkeeper immediately throws a ball to one of the midfielders, and the exercise proceeds continuously. This ensures many repetitions at defensive heading by the central defenders.

Heading Clearances With a Containing Triangle

Purpose: To practice attacking a cross to head clear

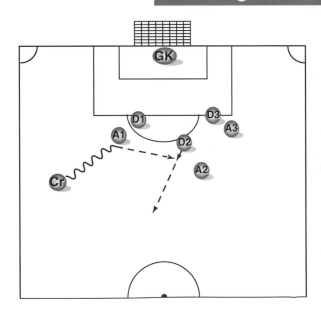

Figure 8.6a Heading Clearances With a Containing Triangle.

Procedure: Figure 8.6a shows defender 2 attacking a cross to head clear. While defender 2 is responsible to head the ball, the three defenders must work as a group to prevent any scoring possibilities should defender 2 mishead the ball or if attacker 2 wins the header.

As defender 2 moves for the ball, defenders 1 and 3 will pinch centrally and drop behind 2 to form a containing triangle. The player heading the ball (defender 2) is at the apex, and the other two defenders form the other two corners. The containing triangle must have good depth.

Figure 8.6b shows a containing triangle that is too shallow, and a ball misheaded by defender 2 goes diagonally behind defender 1 and will be picked up by the oncoming attacker 1. A defender never wants the ball played across his or her back. If it is, the defender will be beaten, as defender 1 is in the figure.

Defender 1 in figure 8.6c is in the correct position, giving good depth to the containing triangle. In this position, the same misheaded ball is still likely to be received by defender 1. A defender always wants the ball played across his or her face, as this allows the defender to close off the opponent from receiving the ball and thus creates the opportunity for a defensive interception.

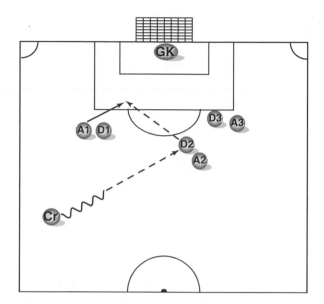

Figure 8.6b Containing triangle between D1, D2, and D3 is too shallow.

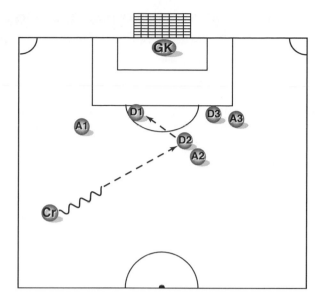

Figure 8.6c Containing triangle between D1, D2, and D3 shows good depth.

Top-of-Box Heading Clearances

Purpose: To practice defensive heading in two critical areas: in the box to clear crosses and at the halfway line to defend goalkeeper's punts, goal kicks, and long balls out of the opponent's back third

Procedure: At the top of the box, three defenders play versus three attackers (figure 8.7). During the learning process the coach may begin with no opposition for the three defenders.

Coaching Points: It's imperative that the coach creates conditions for the players to achieve success. When players are reasonably successful in this stage, the coach will introduce one or two attackers to evaluate the defenders' heading under pressure of an opponent(s). In this stage the coach may stop the exercise to give one player technical advice about heading or tactical advice regarding how the two remaining defenders build their containing triangle. With only one or two attackers, the coach can more easily make clean coaching points. Eventually, the coach will build the numbers to include eight or more attackers and defenders because this more precisely replicates what the players will experience in real games.

One of the critical exercise variables the coach must manipulate is the number of players. In the case of figure 8.7 there are three attackers versus three defenders at the top of the box. The even number means the coach wants to evaluate the defenders' headings in a situation that is close to match conditions.

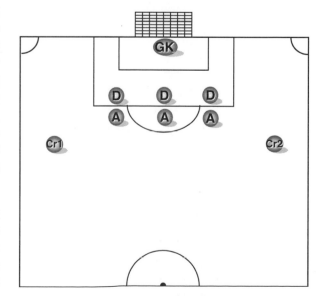

Figure 8.7 Top-of-Box Heading Clearances.

Halfway-Line Heading Clearances

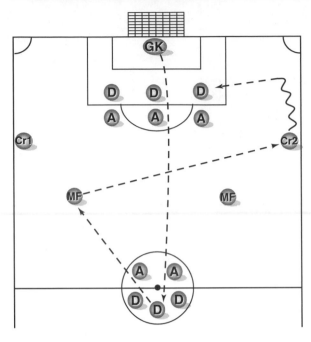

Figure 8.8 Halfway-Line Heading Clearances.

Purpose: To practice defensive heading clearances in a gamelike situation

Procedure: In addition to the 3v3 at the top of the box, three defenders will play against two attackers at the halfway line (figure 8.8). Two midfield attackers are positioned about 30 yards (27 m) from the goal line. Crossers 1 and 2 are waiting on the flanks. The exercise begins with a punt from the goalkeeper to the 3v2 at the halfway line. The defenders at the halfway line head the ball to one of their midfield teammates. The midfield player who receives the ball will diagonally change the point of attack to the opposite crosser. As in previous exercises, crosser 1 or 2 will dribble and cross the ball into the box for the defenders to head.

Whenever a ball is misheaded or lost, the goalkeeper immediately punts to the group at the halfway line, and the exercise continues. Depending on the quality of the keeper's punts, the coach may allow the keeper to move out of the box toward the halfway line to ensure a quality punt.

Coaching Points: The coach again may manipulate the variables to achieve the desired conditions. He or she might begin with no attackers at the halfway line, one attacker, or two attackers—or the coach might even use two of the team's shorter players to elicit initial success for the three defenders.

Variation: Any ball misheaded by the three defenders that goes to the midfielders is a cue for the exercise to become live for a shot on goal. The crossers are always wide, and if played to, they must cross the ball into the box. The exercise is now very much like what the three defenders would experience in a real game. At this point the coach may increase the number of attackers and defenders in the box to even more closely replicate a match. Still, whenever a ball goes out or is saved by the goalkeeper, the next repetition of the exercise begins with a punt to the 3v2 at the halfway line.

Central Defender Heading to Targets

Purpose: To isolate the heading and group behavior of central defenders

Procedure: Figure 8.9a shows a more specific tactical application of heading. In half a field, two full-sized goals are used with goalkeepers. One goal is in its normal place, and the other is at the halfway line. At either end two central defenders play against one attacking forward. Corridors are made 10 to 12 yards (~9-11 m) wide parallel to the touchline. In each corridor are two crossers. Crosser 1 is a right-footed crosser into the box at one end, and crosser 4 is a left-footed crosser in the same corridor but playing toward the goal at the halfway line. Crossers 2 and 3 perform similar functions in the opposite corridor.

The exercise begins with one goalkeeper throwing a ball to crosser 1 or 2, who then dribbles and crosses for the central defenders to head away from the attacker. The defenders will attempt to head the ball to the neutral server or to one of the crossers. When one of the defenders has headed the ball to a crosser or the server, the exercise proceeds to the opposite goal. If the server receives the ball, he or she may serve either side. Likewise, if the goalkeeper cuts out a cross, he or she may serve either side.

Coaching Points: The coach evaluates each defender's heading technique. The heading objective is to first head the ball high, then far, then wide. The most important factor is to head the ball high. Even if the ball goes straight up, this allows time for defenders to reorganize as the ball comes down again. The first objective in this exercise is to head the ball high, far, and wide to a crosser. If that's not possible, then the central defender tries to head high and far to the server.

Variation: Central defenders need to play together as a unit of two. In figure 8.9b, crosser 1 has crossed a high ball that is coming down just behind defender 2's position. Defender 2 does not want to head the ball while backing up because he or she can generate no power to head the ball while backing up. Defender 1, recognizing this, will call defender 2's name and attack the ball with a running start to gain momentum to make a high leap to head the ball clear. When defender 2 hears defender 1 call his or her name, he or she drops to provide cover to defender 1 should he or she mishead the ball. The two defenders must constantly work as a group of two as part of their block function.

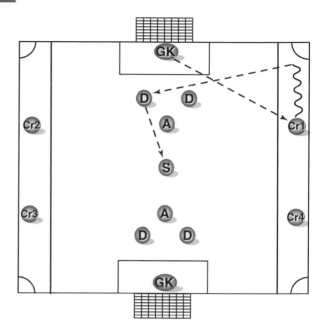

Figure 8.9a Central Defender Heading to Targets.

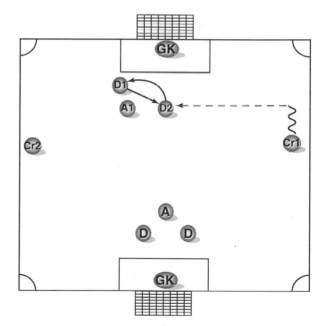

Figure 8.9b Central Defender Heading to Targets variation.

Tracking and Defensive Clearances in Box

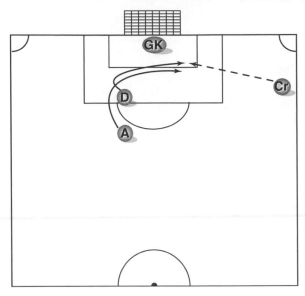

Figure 8.10 Tracking and Defensive Clearances in Box.

Purpose: To practice clearing in dangerous situations

Procedure: Correct positioning of defenders marking runners in the box allows balls to be headed clear in dangerous situations. Figure 8.10 shows an attacking forward who has bent away from the ball as an attack is being developed down the right flank. The defender must mark the attacker by not being so tight that the forward can sprint by him or her. Likewise, the defender must not lay off so far that the forward can gain running momentum to outjump the defender for the header. The defender will be on the ballside, between the attacker and the goal, and a step ahead of the attacker. This positioning ensures that the defender is first to the ball.

TACTICAL APPLICATION OF DRIBBLING

One of the important tactical applications of dribbling is running the ball at speed. A situation in which speed dribbling is essential occurs when an outside back runs the ball from the back to the middle third or from the middle third into the final third.

Speed Dribbling Through the Thirds

Purpose: To practice speed dribbling by flank players

Procedure: The field is divided into thirds. In each final third are two attackers playing against three defenders (figure 8.11a). The three defenders keep possession of the ball until they structure the two attacking players to one side. Figure 8.11b shows attacker 3 changing the point of attack to play attacker 1 out of the back third. Attacker 1 receives the ball just inside the middle third. On receiving the pass, attacker 1 must dribble or run the ball forward as fast as possible (figure 8.11b). Running the ball at speed is best accomplished with the toe down, running the ball with the instep. If there's plenty of space in front of attacker 1, he or she will push the ball well ahead and sprint to the next push. As attacker 1 approaches opponents, he or she will take fewer steps between pushes to gain control so that changing direction or passing is possible. As attacker 1 approaches the final third, tactical options occur. The simplest is the decision to keep dribbling into the final third and crossing or playing the ball to the feet of attacker 4 and running to get a return pass. In either case, when attacker 1 gets into the final third, he or she will make the decision to go to goal or cross the ball.

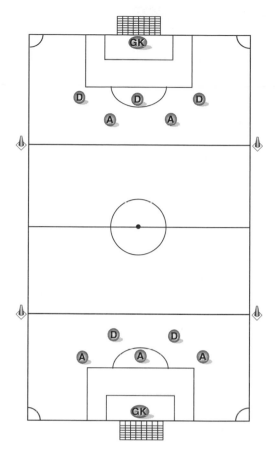

Figure 8.11a Speed Dribbling Through the Thirds setup.

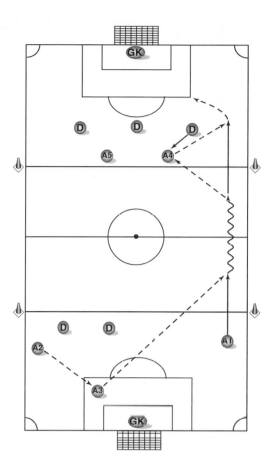

Figure 8.11b Speed Dribbling Through the Thirds execution.

Coaching Points: The coach is always striving to make training replicate what players will experience in real games. As soon as the players understand what happens in a small soccer environment (smaller space or small numbers), the coach complicates the environment by making the space larger (more like the real game) and increasing the number of players in that space (more like the real game).

Variation 1: The exercise in figure 8.11a can be developed by adding a player or players into the middle third. Figure 8.11c shows attacker 1 being played out of the back third by attacker 3. Attacker 1 runs the ball and plays a wall pass with attacker 6 and then continues sprinting the ball into the final third, as in figure 8.11b.

Variation 2: Figure 8.11d develops the exercise by making a 1v1 duel in the middle third. Now, as attacker 1 runs the ball through the middle third, defender 1 runs to close him or her down, and attacker 1 plays a wall pass with his or her midfield team-mate, attacker 6.

Variation 3: The exercise can be developed further by increasing the numbers in the middle third to 2v2 or 3v3. The coach may make an uneven number in the middle third to emphasize a particular tactical option(s).

Variation 4: Eventually, the coach eliminates the thirds restriction, and the exercise becomes a game of 7v7 to 9v9, depending on the number of midfield players. When

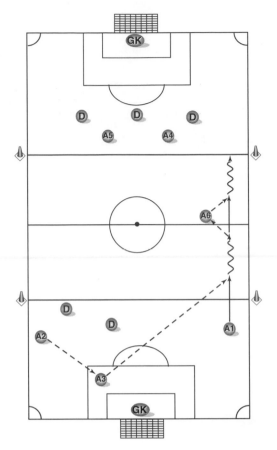

Figure 8.11c Speed Dribbling Through the Thirds, variation 1.

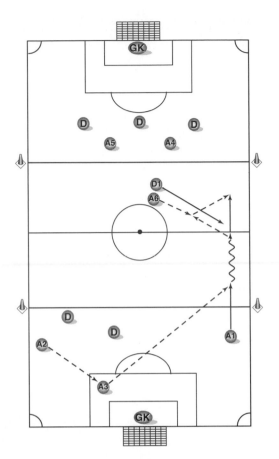

Figure 8.11d Speed Dribbling Through the Thirds, variation 2.

the training session evolves to the nonrestricted game, the coach marks the field to an appropriate size. If playing 7v7, play will occur on a field with goals placed at the top of each box. A 9v9 game will have goals placed on each penalty spot.

In all of the exercises, when the defenders win the ball, the exercise proceeds in the opposite direction. When the ball is lost, the back must run back to defend in his or her back third before the opponent's attack reaches the back third.

TACTICAL APPLICATION OF PASSING

The tactical applications of passing are divided into two categories. The first is passing to players running away from the ball, and the second is passing to players running toward the ball.

A typical tactical application of passing occurs when a back is in possession in his or her back third and a striker makes a diagonal run from a central position to the flank corridor. The position of a defender marking the striker determines which type of ball is played.

Long Passing to Forwards

Purpose: To develop accuracy with the long pass

Procedure: Figure 8.12a shows attacker 2, who is making a diagonal run toward the flank corridor. Defender 1 is not in a good marking position—attacker 2 has outrun defender 1 by a couple of steps. In this situation attacker 1 will play a long pass that is coming down in front of and beyond attacker 2. This pass allows attacker 2 to keep his or her advantage on the defender because he or she can continue sprinting to receive the pass. Technically, this pass should be a driven ball with a low trajectory and the slightest bend. A right-footed right back will naturally have a slight infield bend, but this should not be exaggerated, because the back wants the ball to arrive beyond attacker 2 while he or she is still sprinting and has a couple of steps on defender 1. A pronounced bend or high trajectory adds time of flight to the ball, which allows the defender to catch up.

Coaching Points: This exercise can be modified or developed by adding another striker and marker at the halfway line or changing the number of attackers and defenders in the back third. The coach must remember that the objective of the exercise is many repetitions of the long ball, so any modification or development must still provide for many repetitions of a long pass. In the middle third attackers need to play balls to teammates running away from the ball in three tactical applications.

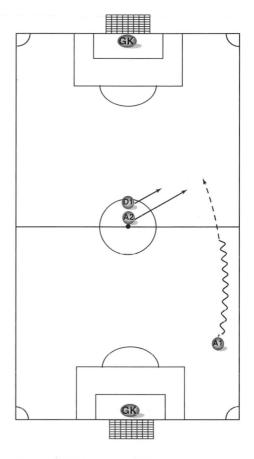

Figure 8.12a Long Passing to Forwards.

Variation 1: In figure 8.12b, defender 1's marking position is much better, and now a ball driven beyond attacker 2 enables defender 1 to be first to the ball. The pass from attacker 1 to attacker 2 must now be played to a space beside and slightly behind attacker 2. This ensures that he or she can receive the pass and keep possession. Attacker 2's team has gained 30 yards (27 m) of territory and is still in possession. Technically, attacker 1's pass should be a softer ball and have a more pronounced infield bend. Attacker 1 thinks of tucking the ball into attacker 2's run.

Note that because of right-footed dominance, many left backs will be right footed. Whenever a right-footed left back is playing a long ball up front to a diagonally running striker, he or she must raise the ball higher to add time of flight to allow the striker to run underneath it. This is not ideal, but the natural bend of a right-footed left back will carry the ball out of bounds if driven with a low trajectory.

Variation 2: Figure 8.12c shows a training exercise that gives the outside backs many repetitions of the long pass to a diagonally running striker. A zone is created in the back third, and the four attackers play versus two defenders. The exercise may be started by the coach punting a ball to the goalkeeper, who rolls it out to a back, or the coach may stand in the middle third and play a ball to one of the backs. In the diagram, the goalkeeper is shown starting the play by rolling the ball to attacker 1.

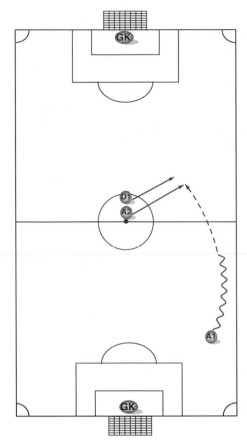

Figure 8.12b Long Passing to Forwards, variation 1.

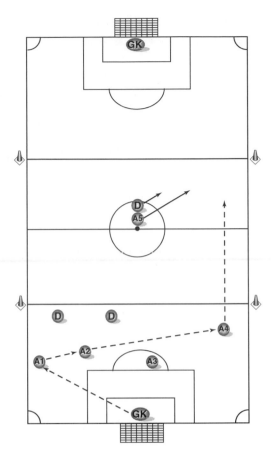

Figure 8.12c Long Passing to Forwards, variation 2.

The four backs play possession until one outside back is played a ball that he or she can serve long. Attacker 4 has received a change in the point of attack and plays the appropriate ball based on the marker's position. The coach may also play a ball to one of the defenders, who attacks the goal until losing the ball to the attackers. The attackers then look for the long pass to the midfield striker.

Changing the Point of Attack

Purpose: To practice setting up changes in the point of attack

Procedure: Changing the point of attack is necessary when the opponents' collective defending action has pressure on the ball and the defense is balanced behind the pressurizing defender. In figure 8.13a attacker 1 has changed the point of attack to the right back, attacker 3, who has seen that a large space is available on the flank and has sprinted forward to receive attacker 1's change in the point of attack.

This is a three-zone exercise with two attackers playing versus three defenders in a zone 30 to 35 yards (27-32 m) from the goal line. The halfway line is a second line, and three attackers play versus three defenders in this zone. Behind the halfway line three attackers play versus one defender. The exercise begins with all players having to remain in their zones, except one of the outside backs, attacker 3 or 4, may sprint forward to receive a change in the point of attack. The outside back may only come from behind and sprint into the midfield third if the point of attack is changed from the opposite side. The number of players in each zone may be changed to accommodate the team's system of play or to make it easier for the players to execute. The coach may use four attackers versus three defenders in the midfield third to make it easier for the attackers to keep possession and set up changes in the point of attack.

Coaching Points: Because defenders always squeeze space toward the ball side of the field, space opens on the weak side. Typically, markers will squeeze centrally to compact the space and cover teammates. Variation 2 addresses these concerns.

Variation 1: When strikers run diagonally away from the ball in the final third and marking is very tight, passes must be made to ensure possession if a penetrating option is not available. Figure 8.13b shows a striker, attacker 7, running diagonally downfield from the player in possession, attacker 6. Attacker 6 plays the ball to the back of the right foot of the striker, which allows him or her to receive the ball with body interposed between the ball and the defender. The striker will be able to keep possession, spin out and play back, or seek a third option. The exercise organization is the same as in figure 8.13a.

Variation 2: In figure 8.13c, defender 2 has squeezed toward the ball side as attacker 6 is in possession. If attacker 6 hits a long ball to the opposite corner, because defender 2 has squeezed centrally, attacker 8 will be first to the ball with time and space to attack the defense. The exercise organization begins as in the diagram and then may be manipulated by the coach.

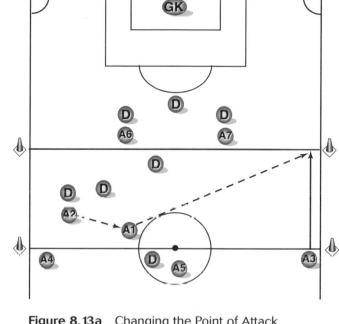

Figure 8.13a Changing the Point of Attack.

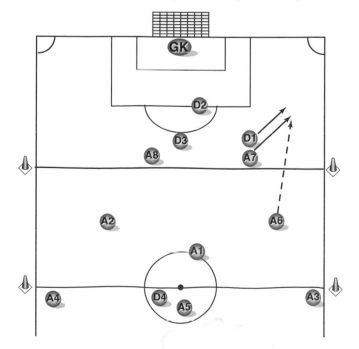

Figure 8.13b Changing the Point of Attack, variation 1.

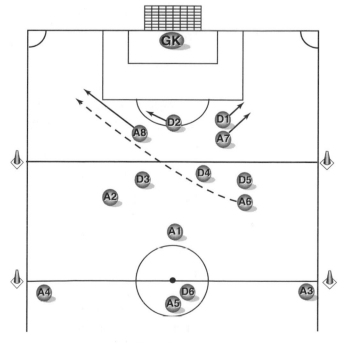

Figure 8.13c Changing the Point of Attack, variation 2.

Passing to a Checking Striker

Purpose: To practice making passes at the proper angle and velocity to the striker without interception by the defense

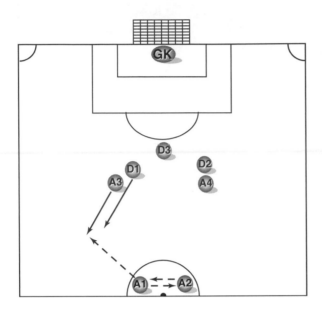

Figure 8.14   Passing to a Checking Striker.

Procedure: The most difficult pass to a player running toward the player with the ball is from a back or midfield attacker up to the feet of a checking striker. The strikers are always very tightly marked, so the weight and angle of the back's or midfielder's pass must be precise.

Figure 8.14 shows a basic teaching exercise for passing into the feet of a checking striker. Two strikers, attacker 3 and attacker 4, play versus three defenders. The two strikers position at the edge of the middle and final thirds. Attackers 1 and 2 play in the center circle. The exercise begins with the midfield attackers playing first-time passes to each other. When one prepares the ball and looks up, that's the cue for one of the strikers to check. It is vital that the striker show at an angle, which allows him or her to see the marking opponent and be in a position to allow a number of options. Showing at an angle also means a proper ball from the midfielders will allow the striker to screen the ball if no support is available.

Coaching Points: The pass from the midfield player must be played at a correct angle. The angle of the pass is placed so that the ball arrives in the space in front of the foot opposite the marker. If the striker can turn, the ball is played to the foot closer to the goal. The correct angle won't permit the defender a path to intercept the pass. The weight, or velocity, of the pass is also crucial. The correct weight should be such that the striker can easily play a one-time ball back to the midfielder. The pass up to the striker can't be too hard because the striker needs time to separate from the defender and slow down a bit to compose him- or herself before receiving the pass.

When one of the midfielders plays the ball up to the striker, the striker plays a one-time ball back to the midfielder. This rhythm continues with the strikers checking, playing balls back, and the midfielders playing the ball in to the strikers. The coach is focusing on the quality of the pass from the midfield players.

Midfield to Striker to Goal

Purpose: To practice passing from a midfield attacking position to either striker who then makes a goal attempt in the final third of the field

Procedure: In the final third of the field in figure 8.15, two striking attackers play versus three defenders. In the middle third, three attackers play versus two defenders. The numbers in the middle third are arranged so that the attacking team has many opportunities to play balls into the feet of a checking striker. The strikers play 2v3 to goal. The coach may permit one or more midfielders to join the attack. The defenders have three small counterattack goals at the halfway line to attack when they win the ball.

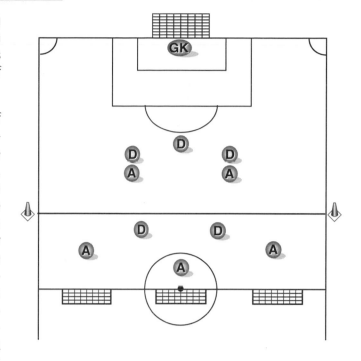

Figure 8.15 Midfield to Striker to Goal.

Coaching Points: As players become familiar with the exercise and have success, the coach should add more players in the attack and the defense.

TACTICAL APPLICATION OF SHOOTING

Today's goal scorer must have a collection of techniques to score goals. In addition to a powerful shot from distance and getting on the end of crosses, he or she must be able to slot the ball past the goalkeeper and finish air and ground balls that come at all angles and speeds. A goal scorer must have the specialized techniques of scoring on breakaways, toe pokes, and screened shots. A necessary cohort to the successful goal scorer is the coach, who must provide a proper training environment for goal scorers to learn and practice these techniques.

The tactical application of shooting is described as *finishing*. Shooting is often thought of as a laser from 25 yards (22.8 m) that the goalkeeper just can't catch up to and that goes ripping into the corner. Although these goals are often spectacular, today's goal scorer must have a wide range of scoring techniques.

Breakaway Scoring

Purpose: To beat the defender on the breakaway and score before the goalkeeper is set

Procedure: Figure 8.16 shows a basic exercise in beating the goalkeeper. Attacker 1 stands with the ball a couple of yards (or meters) outside the penalty arc. Behind attacker 1 is the defender. Defender 1 is either standing back to back with the attacker or is kneeling on one knee. In the initial stages of the exercise, the coach will give the attacker a slight advantage over the defender. When the attacker prepares the ball forward into his or her dribble, this is the cue for the defender to turn or hop up and chase the attacker from behind. As attacker 1 sprints on the dribble, the goalkeeper will be advancing and defender 1 will be chasing. The attacker tries to finish before the goalkeeper is set; if the keeper sets early, this cues the attacker to dribble the goalkeeper. It is always advisable for the attacker to strike his or her finish while the goalkeeper is moving forward and the chaser is still behind. The striker may use a toe poke or bend the ball around the keeper with the inside or outside of the instep. It's important to strike the ball while the goalkeeper is advancing, because he or she has limited lateral motion while advancing quickly.

Coaching Points: The coach will have all players train to finish, but the focus is on players who are in those tactical situations most often. The coach wants a number of strikers and midfield players to be involved in the exercise. Distances and angles should be varied often.

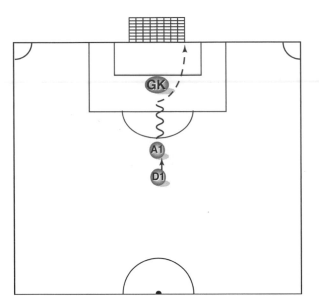

Figure 8.16 Breakaway Scoring.

Cutting Off the Defender

Purpose: To practice cutting across the defender's angle of recovery to intercept the ball

Procedure: In Figure 8.17, attacker 1 and the chasing defender are positioned 5 yards (4.5 m) outside the penalty arc at a slight angle. The coach is positioned centrally and will play balls toward the goal. Attacker 1 and defender 1 sprint toward the ball. Before the defender can get to the ball, the attacker cuts across the defender's angle of recovery to put the defender behind him or her and unable to have a play at the ball. The goal for the attacker is to always be first to the ball.

Coaching Points: The coach varies distances and angles and also varies which side the defender begins his or her chase.

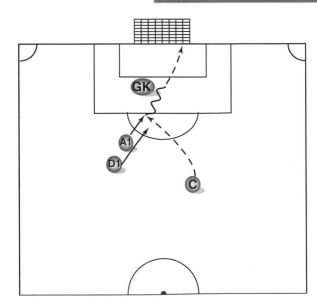

Figure 8.17 Cutting Off the Defender.

Breakaway Game

Purpose: To practice finishing the goal on breakaways and semi-breakaways in a gamelike situation

Procedure: A line is made across the field 25 yards (22.8 m) from goal. Another is made 45 yards (41.1 m) from the goal to create a horizontal corridor. Inside the corridor, four attackers play versus four defenders. Between the line marking 45 yards (41.1 m) and the halfway line is a second corridor. Two attackers play versus one defender in this corridor.

The ball starts with attacker 5 or 6, who plays to one of the four attackers in the corridor. When one of those attackers can sprint behind the defense to receive a through pass, that attacker continues on the break to try to beat the goalkeeper, as illustrated by attacker 2 in the figure. The closest defender must chase the attacker who has broken through. All others remain in the corridor (figure 8.18).

Coaching Points: The coach can manipulate the numbers in each corridor to ensure that the players have many repetitions at finishing. Use fewer numbers if there are not enough chances or more players to make the exercise increasingly gamelike. The coach may also allow a player to dribble if a good breakaway chance is presented. Again, there must be a chaser.

A final stage is to let all players chase into the box if a breakaway occurs. This is very gamelike and should be played to conclusion of a strike at goal if the ball is deflected by the goalkeeper, a ball caroms off the post or crossbar, or if the chaser catches up and knocks the ball away.

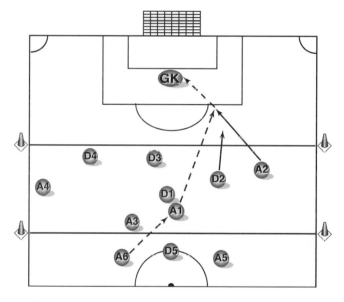

Figure 8.18 Breakaway Game.

Developing Positional Tactics

Tactics imply choices. Tactics suggest decisions. Teaching tactics means giving players the ability to make decisions during games. As with technical repetitions, players need activities that put them in situations in which they must make decisions repeatedly so that they acquire the ability to make those decisions more quickly and more consistently. Training tactics is very similar to teaching someone to drive. You begin by taking a new driver to an open parking lot where there are limited environmental elements to assess while driving. The young driver can focus on stepping on the gas or the brake, turning right or left, and practicing other basic tasks without having to think about other cars, pedestrians, or rules that must be followed. Once the driver has mastered the basic skills, you move from the parking lot to a small neighborhood street, and now the young driver must practice the basic skills of driving within the context of surrounding elements that might affect his or her decision making. Oncoming traffic, stop signs, parked cars, children playing in adjacent yards, and the rules of the road all complicate the decisions that must be made. Slowly, the driver is progressed, and at some point he or she is ready for the fast pace of the highway, where the time to process decisions and make choices becomes very short.

In training tactical decisions, we create similar progressive environments. By taking away pieces of the game environment, leaving only those critical to the decision or decisions at hand, we allow players to repeatedly evaluate and make choices based on the limited information they are given to process. The coach then slowly layers the elements back into the training environment, teaching the player to assess and make decisions within, ultimately, a game environment. It is in this manner that players learn to read the game. Reading the game is no more than assessing the game environment and making a decision based on information that you are trained to process within a fraction of a second. Training players to focus on the proper information often involves asking them questions that get them to focus on the right elements and then providing guidelines for responses to those questions. Every tactical decision has cues that a player must learn to read in order to make the best decision possible. If players are asking themselves the right questions, they are on the right track. The coach's job is, first, to get players to ask (or be looking at) the right questions and, second, to provide them the best response to the answers.

As an example, consider teaching players to move without the ball. Sounds simple, yes, but there are many factors to consider. In a simple 2v2 grid in which the object is to get across the line in possession, the decision process is simplified. First, there's only one attacking player without the ball, so that simplifies the variables for that player to process (just like being the only moving car in the parking lot). The player without the ball can focus on the amount of pressure the teammate is under. If the teammate is under great pressure, then the player without the ball must move in support even if the space is available to run into. If the player who has the ball is not under pressure, then a more penetrating run may be made because the teammate will have the time and space necessary to serve the ball. The player can also find spaces to run into without worrying or having to process where other teammates are running. When attacking the entire line rather than a goal (small or large), the player's decision process is also simplified because he or she does not have to think about a wide or narrow run and how that run will eventually get him or her to goal. The only concern involves space in which the ball is received, because the player can score anywhere along the line. Once players are successful and confident in their decisions within this simple environment, more and more complications can be sequentially added to the learning environment, including more players, goals to attack, offsides in the attacking half, and game time. These factors can be layered in many ways, with the ultimate goal being for players to gain the ability to make good decisions in the fastest and most complicated environment—a game.

This chapter is a brief introduction to the tactical decisions that players encounter as they learn to apply the skills detailed in other chapters of the book. It would be impossible in a single chapter to completely cover soccer tactics. However, by breaking tactical decisions down by position, we can look at a wide spectrum of the basic tactical decisions skilled players will face. It is important to realize that *any* of these tactical decisions could be required by *any* player on the field, but this positional approach provides a framework for exploring the vast amount of tactical situations that occur in the constantly changing game of soccer.

FORWARDS

Forwards are the players coaches depend on to break through the opponent's defense and put the ball into the net. The type of mentality a coach fosters in these players is important. It is easy to create players who will always make the safe decision and not risk making a mistake; however, the tactical decisions of a great forward must contain an element of risk and the possibility for mistake. When working with forwards on their decision-making skills, coaches must encourage the players to take risks in order to develop the proper mentality and tactical ability for the position.

Offensive Tactics: Decisions Without the Ball

The decision of what to do with the ball is often discussed first when describing or teaching the attacking tactical requirements of a forward. However, given that there are 22 players on the field and one ball, I would propose that players (all players, not just forwards) make many more decisions about what to do without the ball than they do with it. So, let's first talk about the tactical decisions of a forward without possession of the ball.

The most basic decision of a forward without the ball can probably be phrased as a simple two-part question: Where do I run, and when do I run there? Basically, there are three types of runs that a forward can make prior to entry into the final third, where runs in the box are part of the game:

1. A run to threaten space
2. A run to support the player with the ball (often called a *showing*, or *checking*, run)
3. A run to create space (a run, movement, or starting position away from the ball intended to pull defenders out of the space the offense wants to attack)

Several cues will give forwards the information they need to make the right choices:

- What are the other forwards doing?
- How much pressure is my teammate with the ball under?

- What is the game situation? Are we ahead? Are we behind? How much time is left in the game?
- What is our team tactical philosophy? Our strategy for today's game?
- Are the field conditions poor? Is the wind strong?
- What is the opponent's defensive strategy? Am I being marked tightly, or are they playing zone?

If you're a forward without the ball, and your teammates are all making threatening runs behind the defense, your best decision might be to check to the player with the ball, making sure that he or she has a short possession option as well as the option to play a more risky ball to a threatening teammate. Showing toward the ball with other players threatening away from the ball also forces the defense to make decisions about which is more dangerous or else compromise their defensive shape in attempting to defend both. When the player on the ball can take a longer touch, the player without the ball can make a run away from the player with the ball and into space, recognizing his or her ability to prepare and serve a longer pass. A teammate under great pressure will need a short option and need it quickly, so a quick checking run at a good supporting angle might be the best decision even when the defense is flat and you can get in behind them.

Some tactics and decisions are in response to the game itself. Others are responses to game strategy of the team or coach. If the coach is looking to play direct (long forward passes) or the team is behind late in the game, the forward will be expected to make more threatening and penetrating runs. If possession is a critical team tactic or the team is leading late in the game, then supporting runs may be a higher priority.

The size of the field can impact tactical decisions with and without the ball. A narrow field means the space on the flank will be minimized, and it will be more difficult to get around opponents on the flank. Players will have to look to the spaces between the defenders for the opportunity to penetrate the defense. Making runs without the ball will aid in the attempt to take advantage of those gaps. Diagonal runs and runs along the edge of the restraining line, which marks the farthest an attacking player can go without being offside, are good tactical options for the forwards to use in this scenario.

The environment can also affect the tactical decisions of a forward. If the field conditions are poor—either due to weather or just poor maintenance—then looking to receive balls played on the ground may not be the best tactical choice for a forward in those conditions.

Great forwards are able to adjust their tactical approach to the game based on the defensive play and strategy of the opponent. If a team is playing zone and dropping off to protect the space behind, then straight penetrating runs will not be highly effective. Short supporting runs to receive the ball in the space in front of the defenders might give the forward a greater opportunity to receive the ball in the attacking third.

Offensive Tactics: Decisions With the Ball

A player has made a run without the ball, received a pass, and now must consider a completely different set of decisions from what we've looked at so far. The complex layers in the decision process here are what make building an attack more difficult than organizing and teaching defensive tactics. A forward with the ball must first make the simple choice: Do I pass, dribble, or shoot? However, each of these options can be divided into further decisions:

- Whom do I pass to? Do I pass to space or to his or her feet? Do I pass to penetrate or to possess? How will I get the ball there? What type of serve does the situation require (bent, driven, or flighted)?
- To what area should I dribble? Should I take space, buy time, or attempt to beat an opponent?
- To where in the goal should I shoot? Should I shoot under or over the goalkeeper? Should I shoot with power or with placement?

There's one important game cue for forwards with possession to consider in any scenario: Is there a chance to score? I think if players (especially younger ones) can answer yes to that question, then they should have the freedom to try to score. Experiencing success and failure is important if they are to learn the answer to the same question in the future. Can they beat the defender challenging them and have a chance to score? Again, if players have a 1v1 situation that could result in a goal-scoring chance, they should be encouraged to take on the defender. Attackers who successfully beat a defender two or three times in a game can be considered extremely dangerous if they are good finishers. The next question to consider is this: If I can't score, can I get the ball to someone who can? This scenario places an attacking and high-risk decision process into a player's tactical set of choices, which is critical for developing the mentality to score goals.

If an attacking player has a chance of scoring a goal, he or she should take that opportunity to shoot. It's knowing what decisions to make following the decision to shoot—the where, how, and when—that makes the difference between shooters and finishers. Great shooters can strike the ball very well, but usually they strike it at the goal and then hope for the best. Great goal scorers make great decisions around the goal. They read the goalkeeper and the defense and time their shots to increase scoring potential. For example, on a first-time shot off a cross, shooting back toward the direction the ball came from gives the shooter a higher percentage shot because the goalkeeper is usually moving toward the far post as the ball approaches. The goalkeeper must then stop and change direction to go back toward the near post. A great finisher uses power when necessary and uses finesse—that is, skill and composure—whenever her or she can. In a 1v1 situation with the goalkeeper, a forward might decide to make an inside-of-the-foot pass into the goal. Technically it's a pass; *tactically* it's a shot on goal.

The desire to score goals dictates the passing decisions of forwards. If a forward can't score, he or she is looking to play the ball to someone who can. A forward who has beaten his or her opponent on the flank (and therefore is not at a great shooting angle) is looking to find someone in front of the goal with a chance to score. As a forward runs down the flank with the ball, he or she must read the shape of the defense, see where the goalkeeper is relative to the back line, and decide what type of action might prove the most dangerous to the opponent. A flat defense with a large open space between the goalkeeper and the other defenders can be beaten with a ball bent into that space. If the forward can get to the end line, he or she can cross the ball by either driving it to the near post (that is, if a teammate has been able to beat the defender and made a run to that area) or, if the defenders have concentrated their numbers at the near post, flighting it to the far post. Ultimately, the forward's decisions with the ball should create scoring opportunities.

Similarly, if a forward makes the decision to dribble, it should be because dribbling creates a dangerous problem for the opponent. A forward who has the opportunity to take on a single defender inside the attacking third should do so—especially if that forward is a younger player, because it will encourage a risk-taking mentality. Forwards must also be able to recognize when they do not have a numerical advantage and should shield or hold the ball in order to buy time while their teammates get into positions of support. Forwards who can hold a ball, beat players 1v1, and finish with composure are hard to come by. Coaches must teach their players all the techniques necessary to execute these skills. They must also teach their players how to read the game so that they can choose the best scoring option.

Defensive Tactics

Forwards are usually outnumbered by the opponent, especially when facing a goalkeeper who is effective playing with his or her feet. The decisions of forwards are based on weighing the odds that their effort might produce a turnover. They must ask themselves these questions:

- Do I have a chance to win the ball?
- Where do we want the opponent to attack if I don't have a chance to win the ball?
- Do I have a chance to put the defender under pressure and create a situation in which my teammates can win the ball?

Forwards (individually and collectively) must recognize when they have an opportunity to win the ball and when they must try to organize themselves to make the play predictable. Team tactics are important here because forwards will be the first to establish where on the field a team will try to win the ball: centrally, out wide along the sidelines, in the attacking third, or in the midfield third. Forwards, when they do not have the opportunity to win the ball from the opponent, must be taught how to pressure in a way that forces the attacking team to play in a certain direction. If a team is playing two forwards against four skillful backs, it's highly unlikely that when the opponent has possession the forwards will be able to organize to win the ball themselves. However, they can cut off the passing options so that the midfielders and backs behind them have fewer options to defend. For example, if the two forwards split wide and keep the opponent from playing serves down the sidelines, the opponent will be encouraged to play centrally.

Forwards must also recognize the opportunities and situations that require a greater effort to try to win the ball. Factors such as a bad pass, a poor first touch, or defenders chasing a ball while facing their own goal are all scenarios in which a forward can abandon making the play predictable and apply high pressure in an attempt to create a turnover. The time of the game, the score, and the field and weather conditions also affect a forward's defensive decisions. When their team is behind late in the game, forwards will need to pressure and try to win the ball in any situation. Field conditions can impact defensive decisions for forwards just like they can impact their attacking decisions. On a narrow field in cool temperatures, a forward might decide to pressure the opponent more frequently. On a wider field in hot, humid conditions, a forward might decide to play more predictably and allow the midfield to condense the space to win the ball in that area of the field. On a dry, bumpy field, the first touch of the defender could be very difficult; this might encourage a forward to pressure, when on a better field he or she might not.

MIDFIELDERS

Midfielders are the connecting point between the backs and the forwards, between the right and left sides of the team. Because they play in all thirds of the field (the defensive third, middle third, and attacking third), midfielders must have a great understanding of how their field position affects their tactical decisions. They must be able to process the tactical decisions of a forward in the attacking third and the tactical decisions of a defender in the defensive third. However, because they are the link between the two positions, midfielders have unique tactical concepts that best apply to the middle third of the field where they spend much of their time.

Offensive Tactics: Decisions Without the Ball

Although midfielders' movement without the ball may not be over great distances, their movement and positioning without the ball are critical to offensive success. Their role without the ball is to find gaps (spaces between the players within a line; see figure 9.1a) and seams (spaces that exist between the lines of a team; see figure 9.1b) so that they can receive a ball with the least risk of interception. For

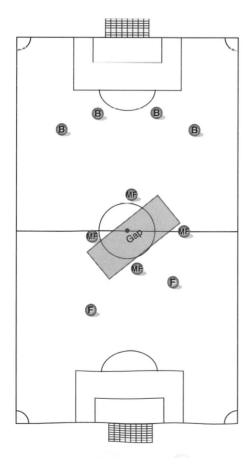

Figure 9.1a An example of a gap.

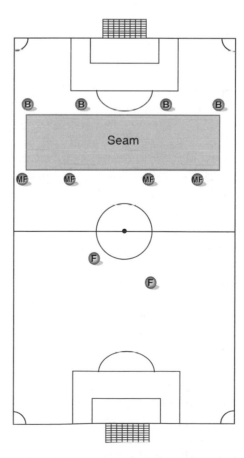

Figure 9.1b An example of a seam.

a midfielder without the ball, answers to the following questions determine his or her movement paths:

- Can I find space to get the ball from my teammate?
- Can I move away from the ball and take a defender with me so that a passing channel to another player is created?
- Can I make a penetrating run into a channel created by the movements of the forwards?

Of all players, midfielders must be most aware of the shape of the team. They must keep the distance between the lines (between forwards and midfielders and between midfielders and backs) consistent so that they can be the link players they are meant to be.

Flank midfielders have the additional responsibility of finding opportunities to get behind the defense on the flank. Wide midfielders are constantly playing a cat and mouse game with the defenders on the flank. They are always threatening to get in behind and withdrawing back to get the ball at their feet or threatening to receive a ball to their feet, forcing defenders to close the space and then making runs into the space behind closing defenders to receive the ball in that space. The wide midfielder must assess the distance and speed of the closing defender, the distance and presence of a covering defender, and the amount of pressure that the serving teammate is under. Although the space might be there, if the pressure on the serving teammate is too tight, the opportunity to serve the ball into the space *won't* be there, and the midfielder must change the run to provide an easier support pass.

Central midfielders can also find opportunities to make off-balancing penetrating runs into spaces that are usually created by a clearing run of the forwards. When a forward clears out of a space, he or she often drags a defender along. This can provide an opportunity for a central midfielder to make a penetrating run into or behind the defensive line of the opponent. Seeing the opportunity and timing the run to stay in an onsides position are critical tactical decisions for the central midfielder. The timing is critical because if they go too early, they'll be picked up by a defender or run into an offsides position; and if they go too late, the gap they were looking to exploit will be closed, and the opposition will be in position to intercept the attempted pass.

Offensive Tactics: Decisions With the Ball

Central midfielders are often the playmakers of the team and, as such, their decisions with the ball are critical to team success. Playmakers determine when, where, and how to attack the opponent. The tactical cues that midfielders must read are numerous, and because of the number of players and the tight spaces in the midfield, the time they have to make those decisions is quite short. This is why the technical demands for central midfielders are high. Being able to deal with the ball in a clean and quick fashion provides the midfielder with the ability to focus on the decision-making process.

The playmaker's decisions are determined by the answers to the following questions:

- Where is the opponent vulnerable?
- Where do we have a numerical advantage?

- Where is there a mismatch on the field? (Do we have a player on the flank with greater speed than the defender? If so, can I get him or her the ball?)
- Do we want to threaten to score? Or are we just trying to keep possession?
- What do we need the pace of the game to be at this point?

The midfielder receiving a ball must deal with the pressure of defensive opponents while trying to find the space on the field in which the opponent is vulnerable and from which his or her teammates are in a good position to threaten the opponent; the midfielder must then deliver a pass to the proper space or teammate. Switching the point of attack is a tactic often mentioned when discussing tactical responsibilities of central midfielders. Switching the point of attack is important, but the purpose is to get the ball into a space where the opponent is vulnerable. When the ball is on one side of the field, the defense will shift and attempt to get compact around the ball. By switching the point of attack, the defense might have fewer defenders and a greater space to defend on the opposite side of the field. Midfielders must recognize this situation and quickly switch the ball to the other side so that their team has the chance to attack the vulnerable opponent. The midfielder, however, must always be reading the shifting of the defense, and if there's a separation as the defense shifts across the field, the opportunity to penetrate through the defense might be the best tactical decision for the player on the ball.

One of the most important tactical decisions a midfielder makes with the ball is the type of service to make into a space or into a teammate's feet. Coaches and players speak often of the *final pass*, which refers to the pass that ultimately beats the last line of defense and creates a goal-scoring opportunity. The central midfielder is often the player relied on to make this final pass. Finding the gap to make the pass, choosing the best teammate to serve to, bending the ball around a defender or into a space, and weighting the pass to eliminate the goalkeeper are all tactical applications of passing skills covered in the passing chapter.

It is the ability to serve a variety of passes that gives a midfielder the ability to control the pace of the game. If the team is behind, but is the fitter of the two teams, playing at a different pace will fatigue the opponent—making longer passes and fewer touches will speed up the game and demand energy from both teams. If the team is in the lead, or is competing in a climate warmer than the players are used to, making shorter passes and using many combinations of passing sequences can slow down the pace of the game, thus requiring less energy expenditure from the players. Players must understand that playing at a different pace does not necessarily mean playing slower. It means making different decisions with the ball but making those decisions just as quickly! Game pace is controlled by tactical decisions, not by the speed of movement.

Recognize that the technical and tactical demands of a great playmaking central midfielder are extremely high. Developing these players takes time, repetition, and an ever increasingly challenging environment.

Defensive Tactics

Basic small-group defending is guided by several defensive tactics, including pressure, cover, and balance. Two key defensive tactical concepts that apply anywhere on the field and regardless of whether you're playing a man-to-man or a zone defense are (1) a good starting position and (2) an ability to anticipate a pass and to arrive as or before the ball arrives. A good starting position depends on team tactics (zone, man to man, forcing the team inside or outside). However, in any situation, a good starting position usually refers to a position on the field relative to your own teammates that prevents the opponent from penetrating and eliminates passing channels into vulnerable spaces (usually the space behind your team). When being trained in small-group tactics, players are often instructed to take up a starting position from which they can see both the player with the ball and the player being defended (which could be the player they are marking in a man-to-man system or the player in their area if in a zone).

The individual defending choices of the player immediately near the ball start with this progressive set of decisions: Can I intercept the pass? If not, can I get to the player receiving the pass in time to establish pressure and keep him or her from playing forward? If not, what passing channel can I get in to prevent the penetrating pass, and can I close the space between myself and my opponent without opening space for him or her to play into?

Players around the ball must read and respond to the amount of pressure that a teammate is able to establish. The following questions should be considered:

- Can the opponent serve? Is he or she facing away from his or her goal?
- Which direction should I have the pressuring defender force the attacker?
- Can I double team without giving the opponent a channel to penetrate?
- Can we get more compact as a team?

In many environments, defending in the midfield is a matter of work rate and effort. Coaches will demand that players attempt to get pressure on the ball constantly. The expectation for constant pressure is unrealistic and can often create a scenario in which players are chasing the ball as a pass is made from opponent to opponent. However, a player anticipating and closing the space between him- or herself and an opponent as the ball is traveling puts the defender in a good defensive position as or before the ball arrives and establishes pressure on the player receiving the ball. Pressure is a critical component to team defending because once pressure is established, other defensive players can organize around that pressure to defend as a group. Pressure is the first tactical concept all players, especially midfielders, must comprehend. Players around the ball must recognize the pressure and respond appropriately—which usually means coming closer together as a unit and compacting the space around the ball.

The role of the player or players supporting the individual who was able to establish pressure is to cover. The communication of the covering player(s) can encourage the pressure to be directional (forcing the attacker to one side or the other), thus making it easy to cover on the side at which the attacker is being encouraged to attack. *Cover* simply means being in a position to defend if the player gets beat or to win a ball that might pop free on an attempted tackle. Players must be taught to defend patiently (not to dive in and attempt to win the ball) until cover has been established. With cover established, the attempt to win the ball won't put the team in a vulnerable position if the tackle fails because the covering defender is now in position to win the ball.

Defensive balance refers to the defensive role of someone on the team to be prepared to defend the space away from the ball if the opponent is able to make a pass into that area or space. As players focus on the pressure and cover around the ball, players farther from the ball must balance the defense to prevent an opponent from attacking a space left unprotected. The depth of that balancing defender (or defenders) depends on the pressure on the opponent because pressure determines the opponent's ability to serve long passes.

Another key tactic to introduce to midfielders is *recovery*. Recovery does not mean just sprinting back toward your own goal. Where a player recovers and the path he or she uses to get there are also choices that midfielders make as they work hard to help protect the goal.

Many of the defensive tactical decisions made by all players on the field depend on the ability to read and respond to the amount of pressure on the ball. Starting position, the distance of the cover, and the position of balance all depend on the amount of pressure that a teammate (or teammates) has been able to establish on the opponent.

DEFENDERS

When your team has the ball, everyone should consider themselves a part of the attack. Defenders have a great responsibility, and the decisions they make when the opponent has the ball can make the difference between winning and losing. Apart from their defensive responsibility, defenders must also understand that the decisions they make when their team is in possession of the ball are equally important. Poor positioning, transitioning, and decision making with the ball can lead to turnovers in the defensive third, which can consequently lead to goals for the opponent. It is important for defenders to develop good decision making skills for both defensive and attacking situations.

Offensive Tactics: Decisions Without the Ball

For defenders, their attacking positions and runs without the ball must take into account the possibility of transition. Defenders must constantly filter their decisions through the question, What happens if we lose the ball?

A defender's movement without the ball is much less risky than a midfielder's, and of course a forward will always take the greatest risk. Outside backs, in taking a position of width to support the goalkeeper with the ball, will usually not get all the way wide to the touchline because it leaves the goal too unprotected if a turnover occurs. On the other hand, a midfielder or forward trying to get wide to spread out the attack should get all the way to the touchline.

A defender's first role as an attacking player without the ball is to support the play and to provide an option to give his or her team time and space in which to play. The defender's movement is constantly forward to get connected to the midfield as the team moves down the field or backward to give themselves more space to play if the midfield turns to play backward because they are under pressure.

Defenders should consider these questions when their team has the ball:

- Can I get forward and overload an attacking space? (This is especially applicable to outside backs, who often have the space available to attack.)
- Are we vulnerable if I make an attacking run?

Making runs out of the back without the ball can be a dangerous attacking scenario because such runs force a forward to track and defend or can allow the attacking team to create a numerical advantage in the attacking third of the field.

Offensive Tactics: Decisions With the Ball

As is true when playing without the ball, defenders must play with a veil of safety when making their decisions with the ball. Ultimately, they have the same choices to make with the ball as the forwards have and the same questions to consider:

- Should I pass? To whom? To space or to their feet? To penetrate or to possess? How will I get the ball there? What type of serve does the situation require (bent, driven, or flighted)?
- Should I dribble? To where? Should I take space, buy time, or attempt to beat an opponent?
- Should I shoot? To which part of the goal? Under or over the goalkeeper? With power or with placement?

A defender does not often get the opportunity to shoot on goal, but an outside back who attacks out of the back (or on the occasional penetrating run of a central defender) must be able to recognize the opportunity and be willing to take the shot. When playing against teams that mark player to player, a defender coming out of the back will remain unmarked and can get to goal for the opportunity to score. If the attacking team attempts to pass in this situation, it helps the defensive team—they will have all the passing options defended because of their player to-player defending tactics.

Unlike forwards, who take risks with the ball in order to create scoring opportunities, defenders must err on the side of safety, knowing that a turnover is dangerous. A defender looking to pass must first maintain possession and then play opponents out of the game by making a pass that beats lines of players. A great rule of thumb for a defender making a service choice is to play the most penetrating pass possible without losing possession. The service choice of a defender, like that of a midfielder, must consider *how* to serve the space and player selected. A ball driven to the feet of a forward must be moving fast enough to get through the midfield line without interception. A ball played into open space for a forward who is running to meet it must be bent with the bend of that player's run—and ideally with some spin—so that the ball grabs and holds a little as it rolls into the space in front of the forward (see figure 9.2a). If there is an opposing defender closing in, the ball can be bent into the run of the player to keep it from being intercepted (see figure 9.2b).

A defender's decision to dribble must be made with caution, but taking space with the ball is an important technical and tactical ability for defenders to have. Often the forwards for the opposing team will not be in position and the space in front of the defender is open. A defender

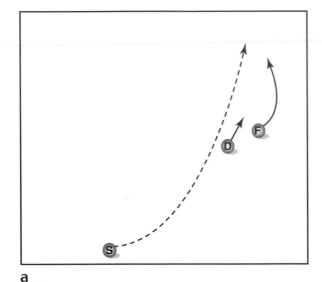

a

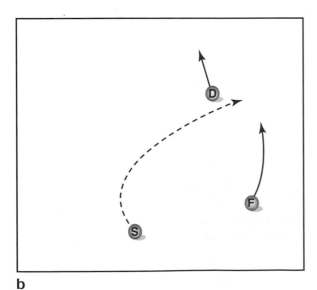

b

Figure 9.2 *(a)* Ball is bent with the player, because the defender is playing tight. *(b)* Ball is bent into the player, because the defender is dropping off.

must be able to recognize that situation and make the decision to penetrate the space with the ball. If they are able to get past the forward line with the ball, defenders again must look to see if players making runs are open or if their runs have opened up the space for them to continue to penetrate with the ball. Defenders must read the situation quickly—if the opponent is in position to deny any forward movement of the ball and the defender attempts to dribble out of the back, the risk of a turnover will be too great.

Defensive Tactics

As is true of the goalkeeper, defenders are ultimately responsible for protecting the goal—a simple task with many complex situations that defenders must be prepared to solve. The tactical questions for back players are many, and answers are often determined by the tactics employed by the coach:

- Which player is the most dangerous at this moment?
- Do I track the player making a run in behind us? Is he or she running offsides?
- Should I defend a player or the space that the player might look to exploit?
- Should I step to the ball and compromise our team shape?
- Should I try to tackle the ball?
- Is there pressure on the ball? Should we collectively drop and protect the goal, or can we step and squeeze the space to put the opponent under greater pressure?

Good communication among defenders is critical because if one defender answers these questions one way and another defender answers another way, the integrity of the defense is compromised. A great defense is one that responds to the game collectively. Thus, teaching tactical decisions to your backs is vital in building a strong defensive team. Many of the answers to the questions just listed depend on the amount of pressure on the ball. If there's no pressure, then defenders should drop and give space in an attempt to buy time for teammates to get back and get pressure on the ball. If there's no pressure on the ball, defenders will have to be more careful in tracking runs because the player on the ball has the ability to serve at any time. With pressure on the ball, defenders can step forward and squeeze the amount of space in which the opponent has to play. Less space means the defending team can get numbers around the ball, put great pressure on the opponent, and create turnovers.

A team's defensive tactics (man to man or zone) play a large role in the individual decisions of a defender. In a zone, a defender is concerned with space and team shape first and attackers second. In man to man, the attacking opponents are the priority, and the spaces and team shape are secondary considerations. The questions to be considered by the defense remain the same, but the answers vary based on team tactics.

POSITIONAL TACTICS DRILLS

The following six activities are designed for repetition of the decision-making processes that team members use while playing. The first three activities focus on tactical decision making in offensive situations. The next two activities are aimed at repetition of the defensive situations and decisions that occur in a game. In the first five activities many of the game elements are eliminated so that one or two tactical areas can be addressed. The last activity (the 7v7 two-zone game) is much closer to the game environment. Using our driving analogy, the first five activities are in a suburban neighborhood. The final activity takes us to the city with some highways and a wider variety of situations. Going through this layered approach will prepare the player for a real game, when making a decision can seem like driving in rush hour in New York City.

Final Pass Game

Purpose: To practice tactical repetition for the decision and timing of penetrating runs and the decisions and technical execution of the final pass into the end zone

Procedure: This is a possession game that any number of players can play. Neutral attacking players can be added to increase success for attacking players. To score, a player on the attacking team must receive a pass in the end zone; however, the player cannot enter the end zone before the ball enters the end zone (figure 9.3). Thus, the player must time his or her run to be moving into the end zone as the ball arrives. The ball must be possessed in the end zone, so the pass must be accurate; bent into the zone, if necessary; and served at an appropriate pace for the attacker running into the end zone.

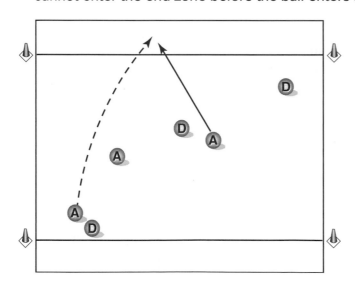

Figure 9.3 Final Pass Game.

Coaching Points: Watch for the timing of the runs into the end zone and for the service choices of the players with the ball, including possession versus penetrating options and switching fields to find space to get behind a defense.

3v1 to Goal

Purpose: To isolate tactical decisions of a midfielder trying to recognize where and when to serve an attacking teammate and the tactical decisions of a forward without the ball trying to create space

Procedure: This activity focuses on a single player's ability to get free from a defender by being deceptive and explosive in moving off the ball. Supported from behind by a midfielder and from in front by a fellow attacking player, a single marked attacker works to get free and score (figure 9.4). Only the marked player is allowed to score and must use the two supporting players, who are restricted to two touches, to beat the defender and get to goal. This drill requires great creativity and technical execution to achieve success. The success rate here—in a 1v1 tactical situation to a single large goal—very much favors the defense.

Coaching Points: Watch for the timing of runs by the marked attacker and for the service options and technical and tactical service choices of the midfielder. Also look for how well the supporting player combines once the attacking player gets the ball from the midfielder and looks to attack the goal. Check the supporting position of the midfielder once the ball is played to the forward.

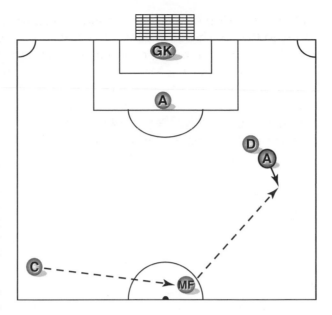

Figure 9.4   3v1 to Goal. (Marked player is circled.)

6 + 1v3

Purpose: To teach supporting movement for players on the outside of the grid and to train the playmaking central player in movement in the gaps and the ability to switch fields in tight spaces

Procedure: Seven attacking players and three defenders play inside a large square grid. Six attackers take a position on the edge of the grid, with one attacker taking a position central to the area (figure 9.5). The attacking players attempt to complete as many passes as possible without the defending team winning the ball. The defending team attempts to win the ball and complete one pass. After three defensive steals (or another set number), the defensive team is replaced.

Coaching Points: Encourage outside players to find the playmaker as often as possible. This is like making a penetrating pass in a game, whereas a pass to a player on the outside is like a safe possession-type pass in a game. Movement of the central player should be in response to the defenders and their movement. If defenders fall in and try to deny a pass, the central player may have to make a run to receive a ball outside the defenders (similar to a seam in a game situation). If

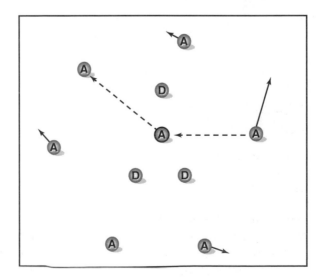

Figure 9.5   6 + 1v3. (Central attacker is circled.)

defenders get stretched trying to steal a ball from the outside players, the central player can find the space in between them (a gap in a game situation). Observe decisions of the playmaker when he or she receives the ball. The safe pass back in the direction the ball came from will keep possession, but great playmakers can turn and play to the opposite side, even with three defensive players providing pressure.

2v2 to Corner Goals

Purpose: To teach defensive principles of pressure and cover, especially to central players

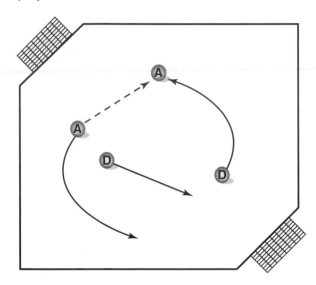

Figure 9.6 2v2 to Corner Goals.

Procedure: Place goals of about 2 to 3 yards (~2.3 m) in width in opposite corners of a 15-yard by 15-yard (13.7 m by 13.7 m) grid. The corner goals simulate a central penetrating channel available from all angles that is vital for central players to defend (figure 9.6). Players play 2v2 and attempt to score by passing the ball through the small goals. Balls that are played out of bounds are restarted with a kick-in by the team in possession. Make sure to have rested replacement players just outside the playing area and keep balls ready so the game flows continuously.

Coaching Points: Focus on the movement of the two players to coordinate pressuring and covering responsibilities. Watch for good choices regarding when to tackle and when to delay and wait for cover. Also look for the collective decision of the two players to drop in and protect the goal when they're not in position to pressure the player with the ball. When pressure is established, players should recognize the opportunities to possibly double team and close the distance between the pressuring and covering defenders. Watch for good communication between the two defenders regarding who is pressuring and in what direction the pressuring player is trying to steer the attack.

Variations: The coach can use several options to make defending more difficult:

- Goals can be allowed directly off a kick-in to force quick transition when a ball leaves the field.
- Players can be allowed to dribble in from the touchline to restart a game and demand good individual defending.
- For quick transition, the game can be played "make it, take it" with a server for each team behind the goals to play a ball in whenever a goal is scored at the opposite end.

6-Goal Game

Purpose: To teach players to defend in small groups (pressure, cover, balance) and to read the pressure on the ball to determine the collective ability to get numbers around the ball without leaving areas of the field vulnerable if the opponent can relieve the pressure

Procedure: The playing area is a grid approximately 50 yards (45.7 m) wide by 25 yards (22.8 m) deep (the size should depend on age and skill level). Place three goals along each end line (figure 9.7). Players can be required to pass through the goals or to dribble through the goals to score. You can put players in whatever shape fits your team formation and tactical system (e.g., four straight across or four in a diamond, as shown).

Coaching Points: Players focus on reading passes to close the space and either to intercept the pass or to get there as or before the ball does to establish pressure. Watch for players' ability to read pressure on the ball and to adjust their shape to get more compact to get greater pressure.

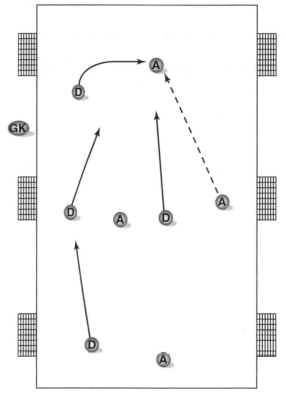

Figure 9.7   6-Goal Game.

This drill focuses on transition—when players win the ball, can they attack immediately? When they lose the ball, can they win it back immediately, or do they have to drop and protect the three goals until they can get together and defend to get the ball back?

7v7 Two-Zone Game

Purpose: To provide a gamelike environment that focuses on service decisions and runs out of the back without the ball for the defenders and on scoring and attacking decisions in front of the goal for attacking players playing in the attacking half

Procedure: The playing area is approximately 55 to 60 yards (50.2-54.8 m) wide by 45 to 60 yards (41.1-54.8 m) long with a midstripe or line to delineate two separate zones (figure 9.8). Attacking players must stay in their zone, but *one* defender can join the attacking zone for his or her team. The attacking players are not allowed to track into the defensive half of the field. The game is played without any other restrictions or rules. Balls leaving the field of play can be restarted with throw-ins, which gives players the opportunity to apply defensive tactics to that gamelike situation. A ball played over the end line by the attacking team is a goal kick. Because the field is not full width, the corners will not match a game field and can create opportunities for the opponent; in order to encourage the defense to avoid the corners, you can make it so that three corner kicks (balls over the end line last touched by the defensive team) equal a goal. To take the next step in the tactical teaching process, remove the midstripe and the restrictions, and make this activity a true gamelike scenario.

Coaching Points: Focus on the passing decisions of the players in the defensive half, the timing of the runs of the players in the attacking half, the movement of the players in the attacking half as they try to create gaps in the defense to attack, the choice to run from the defensive half into the attacking half and how the shape of the defense adjusts to maintain protection in the event of a turnover, and the recovery of the defender from the attacking half if the turnover occurs. Also observe players' shooting decisions—or the decision not to shoot when the opportunity is there.

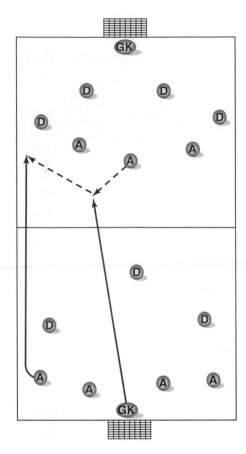

Figure 9.8 7v7 Two-Zone Game.

Coaching Techniques and Tactics

A key factor in becoming a good soccer player is the development of technique. One of the coach's duties is to facilitate this development. Once technique is raised to a level at which the player is able to perform techniques in match situations, tactical considerations can be addressed. Again, the coach needs to prompt tactical ability from the player.

Technique is the ability to perform a task correctly. This ability might involve a variety of levels (how fast a ball is controlled, how far a ball is kicked, and so on), but the fundamental requirements to perform the skill are what need to be ingrained in the player first. Good technique is a prerequisite for good tactical execution. Technique is never perfected, and even the most talented professional will devote a large portion of training to technique. Players hoping to advance their game need to understand the importance of technique. Even the best tactical players will fail if they can't execute proper technique.

Skill is the ability to perform technique during match situations. Many players can shoot a ball quite well during training sessions, but the player who can execute proper technique during match conditions demonstrates good skill. Skillful players are the players we all want on our team during a match because they perform well during a match and help the team become successful—and win!

In most cases, a technique is taught initially. The physical movements for a particular task are given via coaching points from the coach. The technique is taught as a physical task without consideration of the game (no opponent, no time restriction, no spatial constraints, and so on). Match-related components are then introduced in several layers. This allows the coach to see how well players have learned the technique and if they can apply it in increasingly realistic situations.

It's important to remember that there are decisions as to when to employ a skill. These decisions are the tactical element of a skill. The best tactics fail if requisite skills fall short.

Tactics refer to making decisions—a mental process. If a decision is involved, the consideration taking place is a tactical consideration. Often, a gray area exists where tactics and technique overlap (e.g., can I get off my shot in this situation even as my speed is limited?). Tactical decisions force players to know their levels of ability regarding technical execution (e.g., can I properly perform the pass I want to make?).

DEVELOPING TECHNIQUE AND SKILL

To develop proper technique and skill, players must first develop correct mechanics. A player's mechanics consist of correct movements and fluid sequencing—doing the desired motions in correct order with no discernible interruptions. The actions require strength and speed, usually in conjunction. Thus, power is the optimal characteristic desired in the later stages of development A goalkeeper requires power to dive fast enough and far enough to make a save; a defender attempting to clear a long ball needs power to launch the ball successfully beyond opponents. Early stages of development might require de-emphasizing both strength and speed until the actions are learned to an acceptable level. The fundamental movements necessary to perform the task must be learned, and usually these movements are best demonstrated and learned without the confounding factors of time and space restrictions and opponents. Novice players can learn best by observing technique without being distracted from the immediate necessary information. "How do I do this?" needs to be answered before "How do I do this during a game?" or "When is the best time to do this?"

The majority of actions needed to accomplish skills successfully require several key ingredients, none of which can be left out. The success might be singular (successfully kicking the ball where intended) or multilevel (successfully kicking a ball where intended to reach a teammate to score a goal to lead to a victory). The first level of success is to properly perform the technique. The layers of success built from this fundamental level occur to varying degrees depending on the situation. The coach's job is to develop the mechanical ability to perform complicated tasks. Teaching several coaching points together is difficult for the coach—because it's difficult for the player to perform each step correctly. Thus, techniques are typically broken down into small tasks. Each task can be quickly and thoroughly learned before advancing to subsequent tasks. Inadequately learning a task will hinder the learning of the bigger picture—the technique being taught. All requisite skills for shooting a ball can be taught and absorbed, but if one piece is not in place (such as keeping the head down), the technique is not successfully executed, and the ball sails over the goal. The integration of these multiple tasks makes up the complete technique.

Teaching Technique

When teaching technique to beginners, the coach is best advised to present coaching points in limited doses. Beginning players need to master components of a complete action, and they do this by repeating several intermediate steps singularly or in small sets. A young player just learning the game should be taught via small steps, such as kicking a stationary ball before kicking a moving or rolling ball. Successful achievement of one step is followed by introducing the following step or informational point. The coach must know the player's ability to absorb and incorporate information. The coach should know and understand the level and needs of each player being coached. For the beginning player, the coach should be watching for success in the mimicking of movements. Once the player knows what actions are necessary for success, the coach can add further steps necessary for completing the technique. A drill can be repeated and varied depending on what the coach is looking for from a player.

Watching young players shoot requires a perspective different from watching college players shoot. The drills are the same, but the level of execution is obviously far different. The ability to learn and reproduce good technique increases as the amount of repetition increases. The coach should look for players to incorporate good technical information steadily and meet new demands imposed to make the situation and exercise more matchlike.

A good coach knows when players are successful enough at one stage to advance to the next stage. Once players master a technique, they'll want to move on to another. The challenge for the coach is recognizing when a technique has in fact been mastered. Ideally, a coach will know when players need more repetitions, and repetitions can then be provided either via the same drill or exercise or through a new one that trains the same technique. A coach may look to include a team goal

("OK, we need to make 20 shots on goal") and then watch how well the team can perform the technique. This information can provide a standard for the coach to use for future training and provide players with feedback regarding their performance. On this point, players like having a set number of correct executions as a goal because it gives them a precise measure to aim for.

Giving Feedback

Feedback is crucial to help players move from one stage to the next. In the early stages of learning a technique, vast quantities of feedback should be provided. This feedback should be both corrective criticism (when the technique is improper) and supportive encouragement (when good technique is exhibited). For a novice player, feedback can be offered following almost every attempt.

In general, feedback is best presented in the form of a "positive sandwich." The sandwich begins with a leading compliment, is followed by a constructive criticism, and is completed by a closing positive reinforcer. For example, if a player is leaning back too far when striking at goal, the coach might say, "Good run at the ball. I like the way you move forward as you strike the ball. Keep your body leaning forward more as you strike the ball. With your leg strength, you'll generate a lot of power and score a lot of goals!" This kind of comment helps players understand what they are doing improperly as well as feel good about what they're doing correctly.

A large repertoire of drills and exercises is certainly valuable for coaches, but if they don't understand exactly how the drills serve the players, even the best drills in the world might fail. The coach's goal is to develop good mechanics in players, which requires knowledge and experience on the coach's part. Good coaches strive to become experienced or adept in several areas:

- *Possessing and providing correct information regarding mechanics.* Many coaches fall back on their own experiences as players when teaching their players—"We coach as we have been coached." The best coaches have these experiences at their disposal but also supplement their background through other sources, including coaching schools and courses, books (such as this one), and countless hours of discussion with other coaches.

- *Recognizing the amount of information to provide and the sequence to present it in.* Certain skills might be more innate or familiar to players. For instance, catching a ball might be easy for beginning goalkeepers who have experience in other catching sports, so a coach might feel that little direction is necessary for this technique. On the other hand, shooting with the outside portion of the foot might not be as familiar for some players, so this technique might require much more instruction and many repetitions.

- *Assessing the successful application of the information provided.* Can the player do the task? Coaches need to recognize and address the parts of a task players are struggling with. Sometimes instruction needs to be repeated and demonstrated, and sometimes much more is required before players can perform a task correctly and consistently. Coaches need to know what drills or exercises best train each of the outcomes they are looking for. They need to know when to move ahead to the next task and when to stop and start over.

- *Providing optimal feedback to players.* Good coaches are always striving to improve on their feedback methods. Any experienced coach knows that what works great for one player might work terribly for another. For instance, some players hear only positive comments and not the negative, and for other players, the opposite is true. If some players don't respond well to a positive sandwich, the coach might need to better emphasize the particular area or technique that needs to be improved. To stay attuned to player attitude (both individually and collectively), coaches should always be listening and observing—and they should base their feedback strategies on what they hear and see.

In general, the simplest and most effective way to ensure a technique is well learned is to repeat the action. For some, this might mean kicking a ball against a wall for hours, days, and weeks, or it may entail playing countless 1v1 games in backyards and streets. Although the current most common system of training does not preclude this kind of repetition, the standard method of training and learning most frequently involves practice sessions run by a knowledgeable coach. This is well and good, but players should also be encouraged to take responsibility for their development, which means helping them to learn to enjoy the game by playing and training without supervision. A lot of playing time can help players understand how the techniques they have learned in practice are incorporated into real games. This leads to reinforcement of the ideas learned as well as enjoyment. The players want to play not only because playing is fun but also to see how well they have learned and executed a new technique. During free play, the coach should look for good technique and skill to reward players who have learned to employ these in their play. The number of repetitions obtained in a fun session of playground soccer can lead to incredible development in a player.

Beginning With Good Mechanics

Good mechanics are correct mechanics. We all know the cliché "practice makes perfect," but all coaches should be equally aware of the variation "*perfect* practice makes perfect." Incorrect practice creates and reinforces incorrect actions. Players need to make the correct actions automatic. As players master a task, they will become more adept and fluid at the task.

Repetition is a great teacher, but most players require variety in their training. This is where coaches can display their crafts. Feedback that provides corrective information as well as reinforcement of successful actions is crucial at the beginning stage. A player might make a judgment regarding whether certain techniques have been successful. The coach should provide a more complete assessment. Whereas a player might merely see that the ball went in the goal, the coach can help determine whether the steps leading to the ball going into the goal were correct. As players start to understand the steps necessary for successful technique, feedback can be reduced—the quality of the feedback is much more relevant at this time than the quantity. Players soon learn to coach themselves. Following a player's unsuccessful attempt at goal, the coach might ask the player, "What should you have done differently?" If the technique has been rehearsed sufficiently and the appropriate information has been learned, the player will answer this question correctly. This sort of dynamic serves many purposes—it avoids the repetition of the coach correcting the technique, allows the coach to affirm that accurate information has been passed along to the player, and gives the player a sense of control.

CONVERTING TECHNIQUE TO SKILL

The difference between technique and skill must be well understood. Again, *technique* is the ability to perform a physical task, whereas *skill* is the ability to perform a task in a game setting. When teaching young athletes, technique must come first. Match-related components should be added in a progression as the coach sees fit.

Many factors distinguish technique from skill:

- *Speed of execution.* How fast should a skill be executed in a given situation? Do I have the time to take a long touch prior to shooting?

- *Pressure from opponents.* How do opponents dictate how a technique is executed and any necessary adjustments for success? Can I settle the ball before playing it to a teammate, or will an opponent be able to close me down before I can play the ball?

- *Spatial limitations.* How does the space being played in require a different application of technique? Should I trap the ball at my feet or redirect the ball into open space?

- *Psychological considerations.* How do other factors enter into how we should play? Should I play forward quickly because we are behind a goal and time is running out?

When teaching beginners a technique, the factors just listed should not come into play. A beginning player should initially learn techniques without factors beyond the task. As technical ability is achieved, factors related to the application of the technique found in the game may be applied in incremental steps. A coach may choose to teach a technique without consideration of these factors and judiciously apply them one at a time or in combination. Once a technique is learned to the point of being automatic, the coach might then introduce one or more of the differentiating factors. The process of introduction is generally limited to one factor per step. Introducing the new factor typically results in a temporary regression in performance, but as players learn to accommodate the new requirements, the overall level of performance will rise. This sequence of one step back, two steps forward should be monitored. If progress is not made in an adequate fashion or if performance falls off too dramatically, a return to a stage with fewer outside factors might help with the reinforcement of the fundamental technique.

Teaching technique should incorporate Albert Bandura's principles of self-efficacy from his book *Social Learning Theory* (1977). In order of priority, these include:

1. Mastery experiences (performing a task correctly)
2. A good modeling experience (a clear demonstration)
3. Verbal persuasion and encouragement
4. Physical arousal and preparedness

Let's expand on each of these principles as they apply to coaching soccer:

1. The coach makes sure players are getting enough *successful* repetitions of the task(s).

2. The coach provides (or selects someone to provide) a demonstration of the task being done correctly while supplying appropriate coaching points.

3. The coach gives audible encouragement.

4. The coach makes sure players are primed and physically ready to perform the task.

The sequence of learning a skill for a soccer player involves learning technique without pressure (pressure in the form of limited space, time, restrictions, or opponents) and without direction. The emphasis is on the steps necessary for the physical execution of the task. There should be no external factors to deter players from completing the task beyond their ability to execute the demands of the technique.

Direction (such as making the player cross a specific line) is added as the technique becomes learned and reproducible. Direction provides an additional consideration in the execution of the task and is a step toward making the technique a skill because direction is a part of the game.

As players become more comfortable with the technique, a pair of cones or a goal can be included. Obviously, the presence of a goal in the playing area refines the direction aspect just discussed. An additional facet of adding a goal is the enjoyment of seeing a goal being scored. All players like seeing a goal being scored, and this can serve as a great motivator. Scoring goals makes a game fun for players and provides a reward for successful execution of a technique.

As players continue to develop a technique into a skill, opponents can join in. Opposition provides the sense of a real game because players are forced to execute techniques while others are trying to prevent successful execution. Also, opponents can see how the achievement of good technique works to make a team successful, thus motivating them to learn and use this technique when they are on the other side of the ball.

Generally, limits should favor the skill being learned. Offensive skills should be taught with maximum space and decreased as the skill is mastered. We suggest erring on the side of success—for example, provide a large space for offensive skills, and condense the space as the players achieve success. This is preferable to starting with too small a space and being forced to increase the space to allow success—players will figure out that they have failed and require an adjustment to permit success. Reverse the space stages for defensive skills. A similar coaching strategy should be used for restrictions on touch, players, time, and so on.

In addition to a goal being added for the attackers, the defenders can be given a countergoal. More players and more space are added as the technique is polished into a skill. This exercise should develop to resemble a complete game.

Progressing in such a fashion is advantageous for players in that it creates a sense of flow to training. Players can move from one exercise to the next in a logical sequence. Each step establishes a rationale for the following step.

USING TARGET

The steps just described can be incorporated into lessons using the ideas included in Joyce Epstein's TARGET approach from her paper entitled "Family structures and student motivation: A developmental perspective" (1989). TARGET is an acronym formed by the following concepts:

Task—The idea being taught.

Authority—Who is the designer of the practice? Who sets up the exercises and schedule?

Recognition—Using rewards and incentives.

Grouping—Who works with whom? At what level?

Evaluation—Provide feedback and knowledge of results.

Time—A decision that it's time to progress to the next task or that more time needs to be spent on the current task.

The coach needs to *target* a technique or skill and plan accordingly. Several of the TARGET factors require coaches to know their team, including the individual personalities of team members.

Knowing what tasks players need to improve on requires two bits of knowledge from a coach. First, the coach must be able to identify precisely which techniques and skills need to be improved. Second, he or she must know how to develop these skills and techniques. Before a team can take on high-level tactical issues, the team needs to be successful technically. As we've mentioned, technical considerations precede tactical considerations. A team of six- to eight-year-olds should not be expected to be able to change the point of attack with one pass; players at this age lack the physical and technical development to accomplish this. Young players should be able to play the ball to an intended target under appropriate pressure from similar aged defenders. As the defenders grow bigger, faster, and smarter, likewise gains should be expected from the attacking players.

Underlying the issue of progression from one technique or skill to another is knowing when a certain situation holds for the entire team and when it holds for only some individual players. The coach must decide when to provide exercises for the entire team and when to deal with players on an individual basis. Some players don't mind receiving constructive criticism in front of others, and other players do mind. The coach should watch the team attempt a task and recognize if most players are committing the same kind of error; if they are, it makes sense that all players continue working on that task. If only two or three players are making the same error consistently, the coach might want to pull these players aside to review the coaching points. This spares the players from being embarrassed and keeps the activity flowing for the rest of the team.

Clearly, the authority rests with the coach. The art of coaching means the coach knows how much (or how little) involvement to allow the team and individuals. Successful doses of coaching points and feedback will maximize learning and positive experiences for both players and coaches. A coach might be able to provide constructive criticism to player A in front of the group while player B absorbs feedback most effectively away from the group. Again, recognizing and appreciating the fine nuances of human interaction are part of the art of coaching.

Recognizing when the team has earned a reward requires that the coach know skills as well as personalities. The decision to reward the team (and move on to further, more advanced skills) should be based on whether the team has mastered the skills and if an appropriate reward will enhance motivation for moving to the next skill.

It is true that grouping similar ability levels can help advance technical improvements, but it's also true that grouping without regard to ability can challenge lesser players to raise their level to the rest of the group. Observing how well a player performs when leading a group or when facing the challenge of successful competitors can help coaches tremendously in assessing the player. Constant assessing and reassessing help coaches learn whether or not they are influencing the development of the team and the players.

The coach should always be evaluating the team, both collectively and individually. This is a daily task. Providing feedback and corrective information is the purpose of a coach's existence. It's the choosing of the most optimal method for accomplishing these tasks that requires the coach to be an artisan.

Finally, it's up to the coach to decide if the team is ready to advance in training. Of course this also requires the coach to determine when a task or topic needs to be reviewed or reinforced.

A coach is planning not only the next day's session but also the next month's sessions. Use of the TARGET system helps the long-term process flow and makes each individual session effective.

Coaches should be reminded that patience is required for development. Players need training to acquire and to reinforce technique and skill. Some coaches think that instruction and demonstration should be enough for a player to perform a skill correctly and consistently, but this is rarely true. Players usually need to perform the skill themselves, and many times, before the skill can be used effectively in games.

Finally, coaches need to remember that players play to have fun. When planning their training sessions, coaches should always be sure to add enjoyment. If you polled coaches, most would say that when the coach has fun, the players have fun. Keeping this simple principle in mind can help foster an enjoyable and productive learning environment.

USING EXERCISES, DRILLS, AND GAMES

Another old coaching cliché holds that "drills build skills." Well, like many clichés, this one happens to be true. Good drills properly administered promote successful technique and skill acquisition as well as confidence and esteem. The coach's task is to develop a repertoire of drills, exercises, and games. Equally as important, the coach must possess the ability to know the optimal application—what drills and exercises will lead to the highest level of development of players in a given situation. In some situations, a game might be the best method for developing a skill. At other times, or with other techniques, an exercise or drill might be best for player development.

The purpose of an exercise or drill might vary depending on the needs of the team. For instance, a team might need work on combining small groups of attackers. A typical introduction of this skill would include the types of combinations the coach would like to see from the players. The selected combinations would then be done without pressure (no opposition) in a confined area. No direction of play is necessary as players work on developing and understanding the technique. In the next stage, direction (to a goal) can be added. After sufficient repetitions, a defender joins the activity. The purpose of the exercise—to improve in combining to beat a defender to a goal—should become clearer and more gamelike as the progression moves forward. Finally, a recovering defender can be included.

As players become more comfortable and successful with the drill, the coach might choose to challenge the attackers by reducing the size of the playing area, restricting the number of touches permitted, or placing a time limit on the attackers. These modifications promote transition from technique to skill and help players develop by constantly presenting them with new challenges to their play and ability to succeed.

A practice or two later, the coach might decide to use the same exercise to teach defending. The size of the playing area should probably be reduced to allow for success for the defender. Reversing the process (starting with a restriction on touches, time, and so on) and removing the restriction as the defender becomes more skilled is the methodology here. By manipulating the variables, the coach ensures that both the technique and its application are well learned. Knowing how quickly to incorporate changes and add factors such as time and space restrictions indicates how quickly a technique can become a skill. Nuances of the game can be treated and brought to players' attention through such subtleties as when and where a recovering defender returns to play. These factors expose the players to situations they'll face in real games and thus prepare them optimally for the matches to follow training. The coach's job is to prepare a team and its players. A prepared player is a better player. Prepared players play more confidently, are more aware tactically, and generally feel better about playing.

As novice coaches become more experienced and effective, they'll know how and when to adjust an exercise or game through changing size, numbers, restrictions, and so on. This is part of the art of coaching. As players learn the game from the coach, the coach learns coaching from the players. A coach will experiment with a new drill (either of the coach's own creation or the adoption of a new exercise) to address new concerns and help the team to grow and develop.

Players might receive many reps but will not benefit if they become bored or if an activity lacks the intensity necessary for development. The coach's dream player may be the athlete who can practice the same drill for hours on end, but the reality is that most players require some diversity in training. A variety of exercises (even if they address the same concern) is beneficial to keep players involved and motivated. An assortment of drills, exercises, and games also means more fun for the players.

Finally, coaches should always remember why most players play soccer—to have fun. Players want to play the game. Of course, the game is also a great teacher. Every coaching session should include time playing the game, both for learning and enjoyment.

About the NSCAA

Founded in 1941, the **National Soccer Coaches Association of America** is the largest coaches organization in the United States. Its members coach both genders at all levels of the sport. In addition to a national ranking program for colleges and high schools, the NSCAA offers an extensive recognition program that presents more than 10,000 individual awards every year. It fulfills its mission of coaching education through a nationwide program of clinics and weeklong courses, teaching more than 3,000 soccer coaches each year. The organization is based in Mission, Kansas.

About the Contributors

James W. Lennox is currently the director of coaching for the Connecticut Junior Soccer Association. Along with 35 years of experience as a college soccer coach, Lennox has headed up international teams, including the United States men's national B team and the World University Games team from 1986 to 1994. Lennox served as the U.S. soccer coordinator of coaching schools and was named NSCAA director emeritus of coaching, having written the original five-level curriculum for the NSCAA coaching school. Lennox led Hartwick College to the NCAA Division I National Championship in 1977 and was named Junior College National Coach of the Year in 1976 and Division I National Coach of the Year in 1984. In 2000, he became the first recipient of the Mike Berticelli Excellence in Teaching Award. Lennox and his wife, Janice, reside in Oneonta, New York.

Janet Rayfield has been the women's head soccer coach at the University of Illinois since 2002, during which time she has led the program to a 41-21-5 record, reached the Elite Eight in 2004, and won the Big Ten title in 2003. A United States Soccer Federation A-licensed coach, Rayfield returned to Illinois after serving two years as a United States national staff coach for Region II. She served as the 2003-2004 president of the NSCAA and is currently the U.S. Youth Soccer Region II Girls Olympic Development Program (ODP) head coach. Rayfield was one of the best collegiate players ever, leading North Carolina to four national titles while setting numerous Tarheel records and winning several honors, including Nike Player of the Year and All-America honors. She also was named one of the top 10 soccer players in America, male or female, by *Soccer America* in 1991. Rayfield resides in Champaign, Illinois.

Bill Steffen is an NSCAA national staff coach and is recognized as one of the top goalkeeper instructors in the United States. His coaching services are requested at camps and clinics throughout the country, as he has successfully trained players at all levels of the game—from Special Olympics players to professional and national team players. Steffen has been head coach of the University of Oregon women's team, assistant coach of the Furman University men's team, and goalkeeper coach of the University of North Carolina women's team and has played professionally in both the American Soccer League and the American Professional Soccer League. He is currently completing his doctorate in Sport and Exercise Psychology at UNC Greensboro. Steffan, his wife, Refilwe, and his son, Will, reside in Greensboro, North Carolina.

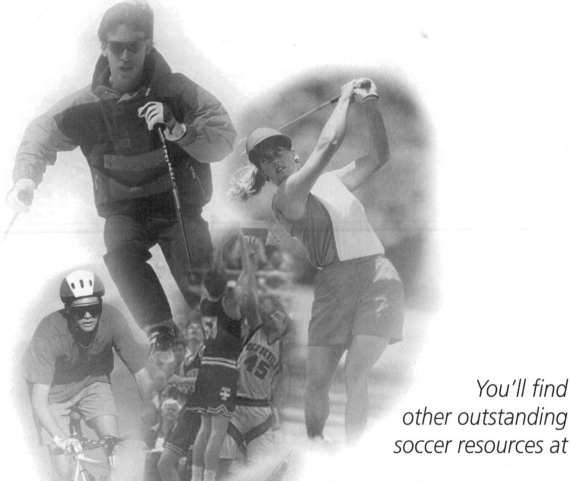